CHRISTIAN PHILOSOPHY

by
Andrew Wommack

Harrison House
Tulsa, OK

Song Boundless Love cathedrals

Table of Contents

Part I

Part II

Part I
Chapter 1
What Is Christian Philosophy?

Everyone has a philosophy—whether you realize it or not. A philosophy is simply the basic set of ideas, beliefs, and values that you live by. It's your outlook, or the filter through which you view life. Every piece of information that comes to you and every situation you face is filtered through your philosophy. In a sense, your philosophy predetermines your response to the things happening around you and the results you see in life. Yet many people are unaware of their philosophy. They have never combined their separate beliefs into a single value system through which they view the world and interpret life.

Pessimism and optimism are two simple examples of opposite philosophies. Pessimists look toward the future and expect the worst, while optimists hope for the best. You could sit a pessimist and an optimist side by side, expose them to identical circumstances, and the optimist would find some positive way to spin what has happened, while the pessimist would focus on the negative. The optimist would look for some opportunity to take advantage of the situation, while the pessimist would focus on the negative and be more likely to get depressed and discouraged.

Philosophy is the reason identical situations can produce completely different responses in different people. Your philosophy filters every experience you have and every piece of information that comes your way. The apostle Paul emphasized this truth to the Colossians when he warned them to be on the lookout for anyone who would "spoil" them through philosophy. A wrong philosophy causes wrong responses to circumstances, and it can cause you to draw wrong conclusions about events and information in life. Christians need a philosophy that is modeled after Christ, and not after the traditions of men, vain deceit, or the principles of this world.

> *Beware lest any man spoil you through philosophy and vain deceit, after the tradition of men, after the rudiments of the world, and not after Christ.*
>
> *Colossians 2:8*

The believers in Colossae learned about Christ from Epaphras, not from Paul. We know Paul hadn't preached to the Colossians in person before he wrote to them because he stated that he hadn't yet seen the Colossians face-to-face (Colossians 2:1). The Colossians were once removed from Paul's teaching, so he wanted to make sure they fully understood the doctrine of Christ. He didn't want them lacking in any area or at risk for being led away by false teaching (Colossians 2:4).

Then Paul writes, "As ye have therefore received Christ Jesus the Lord, so walk ye in him" (Colossians 2:6). This verse has had a major impact on my life. The way we receive salvation is by putting faith in Jesus; Paul says this is the same way we receive everything else we need as Christians (healing, deliverance, provision, etc). It's amazing how people begin their Christian walk by putting faith in what Jesus did for them, but then start thinking they are going to be perfected by their own holiness and good works. You can't get saved by the grace of God and then try to earn all of salvation's benefits through your own effort—it won't work.

Though Paul was writing to Christians, he had never ministered to the Colossians directly and he wanted to make sure they had everything they needed to live the abundant lives God intended for them. This has direct application for us today because many people, if not most, who have been born again have not heard the true Gospel. They haven't heard all of the things they need to know in order to prosper and really walk in victory. I don't think there can really be any debate about that when you compare the way people in the Bible experienced victory versus the experience of the average Christian today. The Christian message being proclaimed today is not producing the same degree of victory in the lives of those who hear it as it did during New Testament times. In part, I believe this is because churches aren't teaching the same Gospel that was taught in the first century.

As a whole, the church has discontinued teaching and making disciples, and is now simply producing converts. Most efforts are aimed at just trying to get people born again so they can go to heaven when they die, but not a lot of energy is aimed at helping converts become true followers of Christ. Yet Jesus commanded us to make disciples, not converts. He said,

we can't keep doing the same thing and expect different results —Janet Parchall

> *Go ye therefore, and teach all nations, baptizing them in the*
> *name of the Father, and of the Son, and of the Holy Ghost:*
> *Teaching them to observe all things whatsoever I have*
> *commanded you: and, lo, I am with you always, even unto the*
> *end of the world. Amen.*
>
> *Matthew 28:19-20*

The Lord told us to teach people to observe "all things," yet the modern church has basically reduced Christianity to confessing Jesus as Lord in order to avoid going to hell, which is only a portion of the Gospel. This is exactly what Paul was warning the Colossians against. He warned them to beware in case they didn't get the full truth, because it would make them susceptible to all of the ways Satan tries to steal the benefits of the Word of God. Paul's advice is just as applicable to us today as it was 2,000 years ago.

The English word **"beware"** in that verse is defined by *The Houghton Mifflin American Heritage Electronic Dictionary as* "To be on guard (against); be wary (of)." It comes from the two Middle English words "be" and "war" which, when put together, signify "to be at war." This word reminds me of standing guard duty when I was in the Army. Some people didn't take guard duty seriously and they would sleep through their whole shift, but I couldn't do that. We were in a war, and sleeping through guard duty put everyone's life at risk. In a spiritual sense, many Christians are not heeding Paul's warning to "beware lest any man spoil you through philosophy." They don't know we are in a spiritual battle and Satan is attacking our values every day. He is trying to get us away from the godly way of looking at things that is established in the Word of God.

We are being pressured every hour of every day, and I believe the attack on Christian values is greater now than it has been at any other time in history. Prior to the information age, Christians were able to isolate themselves, in a sense. They didn't have to expose themselves to the things that were going on in the world. But now, we live in the information age. Television, radio, print news, cell phones, and the Internet are continuously parading the problems and philosophies of the world in front of us. We are being bombarded with the negative philosophy and thoughts of this world more than any generation of Christians that has ever lived, so it is especially important for us to be on our guard.

During the war in Vietnam, I was stationed on a small fire support base that was 41 miles from the nearest U.S. military installation. A fire support base is an isolated base that provides artillery support to soldiers patrolling beyond the range of their base camps. Somebody said that war consists of long periods of boredom sprinkled with a few moments of sheer terror—and that pretty much sums up the experience I had. Nothing would happen for a long time, and then suddenly we would come under attack.

I spent my 21st birthday in Vietnam, and it was one of the days we came under attack. We took multiple direct hits on the bunker I was in and I could see the muzzle fire from our enemies' weapons. On nights like that, I can guarantee you nobody was sleeping on guard duty. They took things seriously because they knew that the enemy was out there trying to kill us.

Christians need to get the same sense of vigilance; we need to recognize that we are under attack. Satan is coming against us and we need to "beware lest any man spoil" us. Spoil means to carry off the plunder of war, or to carry a person off as a captive and slave.[1] In a battle, the victor strips the one he has vanquished of everything valuable, so Paul is using military terms to say, "Beware lest Satan take from you some of the things that God has given you!" God has already given us everything that pertains to life and godliness through knowing and having intimate relationship with Jesus Christ (2 Peter 1:3-4), but we won't experience those benefits if we allow the world to seduce us into viewing life from an ungodly, unbiblical perspective.

God says that you've already been healed. He has already blessed you. You already have wisdom in abundance. You already have faith. You already have forgiveness. Yet many people aren't experiencing the blessings of God because they believe the lies society is being bombarded with, and it is robbing them of victory. They aren't experiencing joy, peace, and prosperity. Christians are missing out on what Jesus has purchased for them because they haven't recognized that we are in a battle. Satan has come into many people's lives and led them away captive, exactly as Paul warned he would "through philosophy and vain deceit, after the

---

[1] Thayer and Smith, "Greek Lexicon entry for Sulagogeo," *The KJV New Testament Greek Lexicon*, http://www.biblestudytools.com/lexicons/greek/kjv/sulagogeo.html (accessed August 2, 2012).

tradition of men, after the rudiments of the world, and not after Christ."

The devil doesn't overpower Christians—because he can't. With Adam and Eve, he didn't use the strongest animal in the Garden to force Adam and Eve to submit to him and eat of the fruit of the tree of the knowledge of good and evil. He didn't use a lion to overcome them and force them to obey. No, what he did was come against them with words, with thoughts, and he corrupted their way of thinking. That's how original sin entered into this earth. That is exactly the point Paul was making to the Colossians. He was telling them to look out lest somebody rob them of what Jesus has provided, by seducing them with words and thoughts that would corrupt their way of thinking. Not just individual thoughts, but enough to change your entire outlook on life, your worldview.

Satan comes against us through philosophy and vain deceit, which means he uses lies and deception. Sin wouldn't have entered the world if Adam and Eve had recognized Satan was using the serpent to deceive them.

Paul goes on to say that we can be spoiled by "the traditions of men." Traditions are tied in with our philosophy; they are ways of thinking and behavior that are handed down from generation to generation. It is the handing down of opinions, doctrines, practices, rites, and customs from one generation to another.[2] Obviously,

---

[2] William Dwight Whitney and Benjamin E. Smith, "Dictionary entry for tradition," *The Century Dictionary*, (New York: The Century Company, 1910).

secular traditions present an ungodly perspective, and are therefore an obvious threat to seduce Christians, but religious traditions can also keep us from experiencing God's best. Not every religious opinion, doctrine, and custom that works its way into the church comes from God—some of them come from people who are mistaken, or worse, self-seeking and deceitful.

During one debate with the Pharisees, Jesus told them they were, "Making the word of God of none effect through your tradition, which ye have delivered: and many such like things do ye" (Mark 7:13). The Pharisees were the religious leaders of the day. They were trying to serve God and by all outward appearances they were, yet they made their traditions—all of the customs and opinions they had added to the Word of God—equal to God's Word. Jesus said that by elevating their traditions above the Word of God, they neutralized the positive power of His Word.

The world, and even the church, is full of philosophies, vain deceit, and traditions of men that will carry you away captive if you aren't careful. They will rob you of the blessings that Jesus purchased with His atonement. One of my goals is to expose those philosophies for what they are: deception from the enemy. Religious and secular traditions have corrupted our way of thinking, and everything in the Christian life revolves around the way you think. Proverbs 23:7 reminds us,

For as he thinketh in his heart, so is he...

This verse stresses the important of what you think at the heart level—not at surface level. Surface level knowledge is like the information you acquire when you go to school and learn stuff just to pass a test, but it never impacts you in a significant way. You might not even really believe what you learned. Back in school, we stored that information in our short-term memory so that we could pass a test, but there's no way we could still pass those tests today. It was information we never meditated on or used, and it didn't go down to the heart level.

Heart-level knowledge is different. Scripture says that as you think in your heart, that's the way you are. In other words, your life is going in the direction of your dominant thoughts, or your dominant philosophy. This is not referring to individual thoughts, but rather the pattern or model you have combined your opinions and life experiences into, which then shapes how you view the world. This is how your philosophy ends up determining your response to life and how you will act.

I knew a woman who came out of an abusive marriage and the experience left her with a chip on her shoulder. She had unresolved hurts and pains that shaped her way of thinking. Her basic philosophy was that all men were out to get her. No doubt, at one time that attitude helped her avoid abuse from her ex-husband, but her outlook continued to influence her even after she got out of the abusive relationship. She didn't trust men, and she was always expecting men to do bad things, so she was sensitive to the slightest provocations. Her philosophy prevented her from having any sort of meaningful relationship with other men, which meant she couldn't keep a job. She had a wrong way of thinking that was robbing her of joy and peace in life. People might not use the term "philosophy" to describe her outlook, but that's exactly what it was.

"Beware!" Paul says, because if you let circumstances in this life affect you and create a perspective in you that is different from God's outlook, then your wrong perspective is going to rob you of happiness and success. Once you establish a philosophy that causes you to prejudge situations, the same circumstances that caused you to come up with the philosophy in the first place are going to follow you wherever you go. You will filter everything that happens in your life through your philosophy, and it will make you prejudiced to see, hear, and find what you are looking for. You'll form opinions, make decisions, and base your actions on the things that are happening around you, but if your philosophy is incorrect, then your conclusions are going to be wrong. This is exactly what we see happening with so many people today.

A lot of people wish they could be different. They wish they could maintain healthy relationships with other people, for instance, but they just can't seem to get along with others. It doesn't matter how well a relationship starts off, something inside tells them it's going to fall apart. Relationships have always fallen apart for them, so they have come to expect it. In order to get different results, they need to change the way they think. As long as you maintain a way of thinking in your heart, then your philosophy will dictate the results you see. This is exactly what Scripture means when it says: "For as he thinketh in his heart, so is he."

Your life is going in the direction of your dominant thoughts. If you can't maintain relationships, then I guarantee you have a wrong philosophy that is causing those results. If you can't succeed in business, even when you have ability and you know you should be doing better, it's because you have a wrong philosophy that is defeating you. Philosophies become self-fulfilling prophecies. If you want to change the results in your life, you have to start by changing the way you think. Philosophy is relevant to our daily lives, and establishing a Christian philosophy, or a godly way of thinking, will have tremendous benefit to you. It could literally revolutionize your life.

Many people know separate truths from God's Word, but they don't combine the truths into a way of thinking that impacts their overall outlook on life; that's why I joke that most people don't let the Bible get in the way of what they believe. They are just tagging on truth after truth to some sort of hodgepodge system of thought, but there is no organization, no intentional effort to create a godly worldview. In other words, many believers do not have a solid Christian philosophy—they have a jumble of unorganized thoughts.

Simply tacking on more and more separate truths to a wrong philosophy isn't going to create a godly worldview. This is why some people can go to church for decades and memorize half of the Bible but never see any real fruit in their lives. You have to allow God's Word to get down to the foundation of your philosophy, and to do that you must make a deliberate effort to change the way you think. You have to renew your mind (Romans 12:1-2).

A while back, we had a woman at Charis Bible College who was in her late sixties and had been raised by parents who struggled through the Great Depression. After living through the Depression, her parents carried the fear that there might be another total economic collapse, and they instilled the same philosophy in their daughter. When the woman came to our Bible college she had a lot of money, but she still had a poverty mentality. She would squeeze every nickel and get every last drop of product out of every jar in the house. It's good to be economical, but you can also get out of balance by being too frugal. A poverty mentality like that comes from fear, and it will rob you of peace in your life.

The woman came to me one day and said, "I've heard all of your teachings on prosperity, and intellectually I understand what you're saying. I see that I should be more generous and I shouldn't be afraid, but this is the way I was raised." What she was saying was that she knew her philosophy was wrong, but she felt like she couldn't change the way she looked at life.

Changing the way you think is hard, and it isn't necessarily going to change simply because you are presented with the truth. Individual truths are not going to change your philosophy unless you make the effort to embrace those truths. The Word says, "And ye shall know the truth, and the truth shall make you free" (John 8:32), but it's only the truth you *know* that sets you free. To be set free, you have to have more than a mere mental awareness of truth, you need a heart-level understanding.

16

What Is Christian Philosophy?

Recently, I was talking to some friends who told me they know people who have studied every one of my teachings, and they study the Word, but they still aren't operating in faith. They can quote all of the things I say about trusting God, but they don't trust God. The truths they have learned haven't changed their philosophy, and I think that's tragic. You have to get beyond merely possessing individual pieces of information. You need more than facts to be set free. You have to combine those facts, connect the dots, and pull them all together so that they change the way you look at life.

We have a tendency to think that our problems are our problem, but they aren't. Often, our problems are just symptoms of deeper heart issues. We're looking for physical or natural reasons to explain why our life is the way it is, but the condition of our lives is a result of the way we think—not what is going on around us. Outside forces have an impact on us for sure, but they aren't the determining factor in our reality. The apostle Paul said, "We are troubled on every side, yet not distressed; we are perplexed, but not in despair; persecuted, but not forsaken; cast down, but not destroyed" (2 Corinthians 4:8-9). The way we respond to what happens to us determines the condition of our lives, and the way we respond is a direct result of our philosophy.

I have seen this very clearly in some of the third world countries in which I've ministered. The poverty is so severe, you want to just throw money at the problem. But others have done that and the people are still struggling. I've come to realize they struggle because of their philosophy. You can't just give people a fish, you need to teach them to fish. If you just give money to people who have a poverty attitude, they will quickly be poor again. They need a new way of thinking; a new philosophy.

The most important thing you will ever do is renew your mind and form a Christian philosophy, or a Christian worldview. Once you have a Christian way of looking at things, then your philosophy becomes a filter through which you see and experience life. Everything gets filtered through what God has said and you see the positive instead of the negative. You'll be encouraged when other people are panicking. You'll operate in faith when other people are running scared.

Whether you realize it or not, you have a philosophy, or a way of looking at life. It's an attitude that has been formed by the way you were brought up, by the experiences you've had, and by the things you've learned. Through all of those things, you have formed a way of seeing life that largely predetermines your responses, and even your experience of life.

Right now, we're in an economic downturn. Other people with a less optimistic philosophy, are calling it a worldwide financial crisis. News broadcasts are busy prophesying doom, gloom, and disaster. I don't deny the economic challenges out there, but I'm not a pessimist either. I'm not fearful and preparing for the worst-case scenario. Scripture says that perfect love casts out fear (1 John 4:18). If you are secure in the Lord and you know God is your source—not this world system—then you can go ahead and prosper while the whole world is falling apart. It doesn't matter what condition the world economy is in, because the world economy isn't our source. God is our source.

My personal finances are prospering and so is our ministry. While the stock market has been in decline, my portfolio has been increasing. While many organizations are making cutbacks, our ministry is seeing the greatest growth and income we've ever seen. We're reaching more people with the Gospel than ever before, and things are working for us. Our experiences are completely contrary to what the world is saying should be happening.

The reason we are prospering is because I have a philosophy that is based on years and years of walking with God and seeing God bring me through. My faith and hope are in the Lord—not in the world economy. My Christian philosophy causes me to filter information differently than the world does.

The dominant worldview in modern society is humanistic, which tries to explain life and truth purely from the perspective of what matters to humans. Humanism rejects God totally, but aspects of humanistic philosophy have worked their way into many Christians' belief systems. Instead of filtering life from God's perspective, many Christians are filtering life through mental reasoning. Instead of trusting in God, society is conditioning believers to lean unto their own understanding (Proverbs 3:5). Instead of walking by faith, Christians are being encouraged to walk by sight (2 Corinthians 5:7). This is exactly what the apostle Paul warned us against. It is a direct attack from the devil to rob believers of God's promises for us "through philosophy and vain deceit, after the tradition of men, after the rudiments of the world, and not after Christ" (Colossians 2:8).

Too many Christians are looking at life from a humanistic standpoint. They aren't factoring in God as their source, and they feel like they are limited by how the world's system is going. When people have a philosophy that doesn't factor in God, they fall into panic when the stock market crashes, jobs are being lost, and the media is crying about a financial crisis. We've all heard stories about millionaires who committed suicide because they lost money and thought their lives were over. Those kinds of people have their whole identity wrapped up in possessions. People who have a philosophy that God is their source won't fall to pieces in a crisis because their joy and satisfaction are found in God and in relationship with Him.

Putting your hope or trust in the principles and elements of this world is a wrong philosophy. It's a wrong outlook, and the long-term effect is the deterioration of society. A large segment of society doesn't believe in God, and even if they believe in *a* god, they don't believe in heaven or hell. We've taken prayer out of schools and instead teach children to trust in the principles of this world. It's no wonder our society is heading downhill fast.

Several years ago, two boys went into a high school in a Denver, Colorado, suburb and killed 13 people, and then they killed themselves before they could be captured. They thought they were avoiding prosecution, but, boy, did they miss it. They didn't believe in God, and they had a wrong philosophy that led them to believe the end of this life was the end of all existence; so they committed suicide to avoid punishment for their crimes. But they didn't escape anything. What they did was eliminate any opportunity for forgiveness and usher themselves straight into an eternity of torment and separation from God.

It's a lot harder to get guns today than it was fifty years ago, but we never had shooting incidents in schools back then. Now, we have policemen and metal detectors in schools, but we're seeing terrible violence. It has nothing to do with gun restrictions. It has to do with the removal of moral restrictions as a result of the ungodly worldviews being promoted in society today. It's a philosophy issue.

Everywhere you look there is a new group trying to pass more laws in an attempt to control the way people behave. Some are even trying to pass laws about fatty foods and what is, or isn't, acceptable to eat. For the most part, those people don't have a godly worldview, and they think the answer to society's problems is to create more legal restrictions and punishments. In the absence of Christian philosophy they are trying to come up with controls to limit immorality, but that is the wrong approach. Society doesn't need more laws; the people in society need to embrace morality—specifically, a biblically based way of thinking.

Satan is destroying individuals and societies by leading people captive through ungodly philosophies and traditions. You'd think all Christians would understand the need to have an outlook that conforms to the Word of God, but I'm amazed how many believers don't seem to get this. Everyone wants to be politically correct. People don't want to tell anybody else that they are wrong, or that it is immoral to act in certain ways. The irony is that in a society where everyone is free to act however they want, the government is forced to intrude more and more into civil liberties in order to restrict unwanted behaviors. People without moral restraint have to be controlled by other means.

Unfortunately, you can see this process taking place in the United States and other Western countries. Some people seem to think that being free means being liberal in the way you think, but that's not true. We have to control the way we think. The way people act is a result of how they think, and a thought process that says everything is permissible promotes immoral behavior, which then leads to the deterioration of society.

When the apostle Paul warned against being spoiled through philosophy, vain deceit, the traditions of men, and the rudiments of this world, he was saying, "Don't think like a lost person. Don't think the way the world thinks." We need a biblical philosophy.

The world is filled with people who have no relationship with God, and therefore they have a very ungodly philosophy. People who think according to the principles of this world say God doesn't exist, and they believe humans evolved by accident over billions of years. They don't acknowledge God, and they don't understand that we were created and designed by Him. To think this way is to think like a lost person.

What Is Christian Philosophy?

The world's way of thinking is not a comprehensive and rational philosophy. For instance, how does a society that goes to great lengths to promote the environment and protect even the most obscure animal species arrive at the conclusion that it's okay to abort babies? The world's way of thinking is a wrong philosophy, and it leads to wrong results. Some of the same people who yell about recycling think that having a baby is a choice, and if having a baby is inconvenient, they think it's okay to kill the baby. Society needs to get its priorities straight. God gave us life. We are not just like the rest of creation, and we are not equal to animals.

I'll be dealing with specific philosophies later on, but right now I just want to show how behavior comes from philosophy, and why having a Christian philosophy is important for believers. We can't afford to think like the world thinks. We need to have a philosophy that focuses on God more than all of these secular ideas that are being promoted. The worldly attitudes being pushed on us go against a Christian way of thinking.

Many believers today are establishing a philosophy independently of God and separate from what the Word of God teaches. I read about the results of a survey that questioned people about how they established their theology. The survey was only given to people who identified themselves as born-again Christians, and they were asked how they formed their opinions. The majority of people said they just come up with their own philosophy based on life experiences and their own way of thinking. One question asked if they adhere to the Word of God as being absolute, and only a small percentage answered yes. Remember, these were people who identified themselves as born-again Christians.

Instead of getting their philosophy from the Word of God, these people were basing it on how they were raised, what they had been taught in school, books they had read, and the study of principles from other world religions. They had established their philosophy piecemeal. People are taking a buffet-style approach to the assembly of ideas, and that's not a good idea. If you do that, Satan is going to spoil you. He's going to take from you what Jesus has already purchased, and what belongs to you by right of inheritance.

A Christian philosophy must be rooted in the Word of God. You can't form a proper Christian worldview without renewing your mind in the Word of God. When Jesus was praying to the Father, He said, "Sanctify them through thy truth: thy word is truth" (John 17:17). I just can't overemphasize how important it is for us to conform our minds to the Word of God, and not to the philosophies and principles of this world.

Unfortunately, a lot of Christians aren't looking to the Word for their philosophy. They have bought into Satan's deception that the Word of God contains bits and pieces of truth, but it isn't completely accurate. They think it's outdated because it was written 2,000 years ago, and that it can't possibly have wisdom for modern society. In fact, some don't believe that the Bible is the inerrant word of God, or that Jesus Christ is the only way to salvation—they say He is one of many ways. That's a wrong philosophy, and Satan will use that perspective to come into your life and steal from you.

Psalm 91 says, "…His truth shall be thy shield and buckler" (v. 4). The Word of God and the promises it contains are our armor and protection against the attacks of the enemy. The Word is 100% accurate, it's totally relevant, and it is the only thing Christians should be basing their lives upon. The way you change your core values and obtain a Christian philosophy is by conforming your worldview to the Word of God, instead of just leaning on your own understanding.

If you want to see the results the Word of God promises, then you have to adopt God's way of thinking. I have conformed my philosophy to the Word, and it's working. My health is great, I'm seeing the miraculous power of God, my stock investments have gained 61% in value while the world has been crying about a financial crisis, I'm happy, I'm joyful, my relationships are good, life is good, and God is blessing me in every area of my life. I'm not bragging, I'm just trying to give an example that conforming your way of thinking to the Word of God works. I'm not special—you can have the same results because God doesn't play favorites. All I've done is put God first and recognize that I'm not smart enough to direct my own life. I just do what God tells me to do, instead of doing what makes sense to me, or what I feel like doing.

Being a Christian isn't about changing your outward appearance. It isn't about what you do and how you act. If you don't change the wrong concepts and the belief system on the inside, then you're going to have the same results in your life you had before you were saved. That's why God gave us His Word—to change the way we think. The Word of God contains His thoughts, His values, and His way of thinking. It's our ticket to a new life.

I don't care what society says is right or wrong, I follow what God says. Society may say homosexuality is just another lifestyle, or that a homosexual union is just as important as a marriage between a man and a woman, but God's Word says differently. If you subscribe to the world's view instead of God's, then the devil is going to steal from you. The world is trying to say that there are many paths to God, and we need to embrace other philosophies. God's Word says we should be on our guard against any philosophy that isn't modeled after Jesus Christ. The world is trying to say the Bible represents an outdated standard of morality; they want to pretend that we've "evolved" beyond the Bible, and now we should just embrace life.

The world's philosophies are simply an attempt by the devil to undermine the Word of God—which is the same thing Satan did to Adam and Eve. The enemy wants to strip you of the armor and protection of God's Word so that he can plunder your life and steal what Jesus has already won for you. Jesus said,

> *A good tree cannot bring forth evil fruit, neither can a corrupt tree bring forth good fruit. Every tree that bringeth not forth good fruit is hewn down, and cast into the fire.*
>
> *Matthew 7:18-19*

The fruit of a tree is directly related to the tree itself. In the same way, you aren't going to get the fruit of God's manifold blessings if your core belief system is conformed to the world's way of thinking. You need a Christian philosophy. If you aren't seeing the fruit in your life that you would like to see, then all you have to do is change the way you think in your heart and adopt God's way of looking at life. Once you do that, the fruit will come.

Conforming your way of thinking to God's Word will bring a harvest of blessings in your life, but they don't all come overnight. The natural law of sowing and reaping means that it takes time for a seed to grow into a fruit-bearing plant, and there is a similar spiritual law of sowing and reaping. God provides miracles when there isn't time to wait for a harvest, like healing sickness, but God's best is for you to walk in His blessings daily. For instance, it is better to walk in health and never need healing than it is to get sick and need a miracle. Likewise, it is better to have money in the bank to meet all of your needs than it is to need a miracle to pay your rent every month. Even after you renew your mind, it may take time to get to where you don't need a miracle every month, but don't get discouraged. Scripture says,

> *And let us not be weary in well doing: for in due season we shall reap, if we faint not.*
>
> *Galatians 6:9*

This means we have to stay focused on God and meditate on His Word to maintain our Christian perspective and reap the fruit God desires for us. If you are willing to do that, and you change the way you think at the heart level, then you will see God's blessings in your life—guaranteed.

I challenge you to prayerfully consider the Christian philosophies I present in the rest of this book and embrace them. It will change the way you think, which will change the rest of your life.

Chapter Two

Why Should I Care About Philosophy?

I went to Poland a number of times in the 1980s before the Berlin Wall came down, when Poland was still under communist rule. I stuck out in my cowboy boots and, of course, the moment I opened my mouth people knew I was an American. Americans were an unusual sight for the Polish people, and they were always gathering around me in curiosity. I wanted to blend in better and get a feel for what life was really like in Poland, so I borrowed some clothes from my interpreter. Then I went out into public wearing his clothes and stayed completely silent so that I could try to pass myself off as Polish.

The interpreter and I started walking down the street and within five minutes a crowd of young people had gathered around me saying, "American! American!" I was wearing Polish clothes and I hadn't said a word, but they could still tell I was an American.

I said to my interpreter, "How do these people know I'm an American?"

"It's your attitude," he said.

"What do you mean my attitude?" I asked. "I haven't said or done anything."

"You don't understand. We've lived under communist rule for over 70 years," he said. He went on to explain how they had learned to be afraid under the oppression of communism. They never made eye contact with strangers when walking down the street because they didn't want to draw attention to themselves. They even took on submissive body language. They didn't walk down the street with their heads up and their shoulders square; they stooped and looked at the ground. They didn't start conversations with strangers, because the person might have been KGB. All of their mannerisms were aimed at being as inconspicuous as possible.

I wasn't doing any of those things. I was standing on the street corner looking people in the eye and smiling. I was nodding my head at strangers to say hello. My positive attitude was coming through without speaking a word to anyone, and they could tell I was an American. My philosophy was evident—and so was theirs.

Everyone has a philosophy, whether they acknowledge it or not, and all philosophies produce fruit. Your philosophy is a filter that determines how you act. When Proverbs says that you will be as you think in your heart (Proverbs 23:7), I believe it's talking about your philosophy. The system of thought that you hold in your heart determines the course of your life. As I've said, your life right now is a product of the way you have been thinking.

People don't generally desire divorce, bankruptcy, or sickness, so experiencing those things doesn't mean you desired them. It just means you had a philosophy that made you susceptible to those experiences. For instance, you could have been thinking, "Lord, I'm only human; I'm just a man," instead of thinking about who you are in Christ and conforming your thoughts to the Word which says "...greater is he that is in you, than he that is in the world" (1 John 4:4). Forgetting that you are a child of God and thinking that you are a nobody makes you susceptible to attacks from the enemy.

The root word "philosophy" that Paul used in his admonition to the Colossians was used in only one other place in Scripture. It was when Paul was speaking to the Greeks,

> *Then certain philosophers of the Epicureans, and of the Stoicks, encountered him. And some said, What will this babbler say? other some, He seemeth to be a setter forth of strange gods: because he preached unto them Jesus, and the resurrection.*
>
> *Acts 17:18*

We are still encountering these philosophies today. Epicureans derived their teaching from the philosopher Epicurus who founded a school in Athens, Greece, around 300 B.C. Epicurus taught that the world is a random combination of atoms and that pleasure is the highest good.[3] His followers soon devolved into a materialistic group; a lot like the materialistic and pleasure-seeking

---

[3] Definition from Princeton's WordNet, online at http://wordnet.princeton.edu/

society that the modern philosophy of evolution is giving rise to today. Having fun and seeking pleasure pretty much sums up most people's philosophy today. In fact, the theory of evolution is simply a new presentation of the Epicurean belief that life is the result of the random collision of atoms.

A Christian philosophy puts relationship with God above pleasure. I have a philosophy that pleasing God is more important than pleasing myself. If seeking God means doing something that isn't pleasurable, I'll suffer the consequences because I don't make my decisions based on what makes me feel good. The world promotes buying the biggest house you possibly can, the biggest car, and indulging every sense you have. The world's philosophy is "Get all you can. Can all you get. And sit on your can." But God teaches that it is more blessed to give than to receive (Acts 20:35), and Jesus said that a man's life does not consist in the abundance of possessions (Luke 12:15). People are more important than possessions, and I want to make my life count; that means I need to be serving others, not gathering stuff together for myself.

The second part of Epicurus' philosophy was to avoid pain at all costs.[4] Unfortunately, pain is sometimes necessary to accomplish good. Freedom, for example, has a cost. Millions of people have died in battle for freedom. A lot of pain was endured during World War II to provide the freedom that we enjoy today. A self-seeking philosophy doesn't allow for sacrifice like that; it leads

---

[4] Andrew Wommack, Living Commentary Bible software, note for Acts 17:18.

people to put their heads in the sand and hope that problems will just go away.

When Hitler began his rise to power, as he first started implementing his racist policies, a lot of people thought he would just go away. Many governments had come and gone in Germany since they lost the First World War, and people thought Hitler would be another passing fad. Everyone wanted to avoid conflict and so they ignored Hitler and hoped he would fade away. Obviously he didn't, and his plans for a "master race" and the genocide he employed in that pursuit plunged the world into a war in which over 50 million people died.

Today, people are hoping our problems will go away just like Europe hoped Hitler would. People are putting their heads in the sand and ignoring attacks upon our society such as abortion and the promotion of the lesbian, gay, bi-sexual, and transsexual agenda, in the hopes that it will all go away. But those attacks aren't going away unless individuals in society make a stand for morality. Ignoring these warning signs is a recipe for disaster. It's a wrong philosophy.

The reference to stoics in the above scripture refers to the Greek philosopher Zeno who founded a competing school of thought at the same time as Epicurus. The stoics believed that virtue was sufficient for happiness, and that the ultimate goal in life was to become free from the fluctuations of emotion—pleasure or pain.[5]

---

[5] From the Stanford Encyclopedia of Philosophy online at http://plato.stanford.edu/entries/stoicism/

Stoics sought to calmly accept all circumstances as the unavoidable result of divine will or the natural order.[6]

A lot of Christians today are stoic in their philosophy. The extreme sovereignty of God doctrine is a perversion of Scripture in that it falsely teaches that everything that happens in life is preordained by God. It's nothing more than a stoical worldview. People who teach that doctrine think absolutely everything that happens in life is God's will—even evil things such as murder, rape, and sickness. Those people believe that even if God didn't cause the event directly, He must have allowed it to happen because He is all-powerful and He could have stopped it if it was against His will.

It's true that God is all-powerful, but His Word teaches that He has no part in evil (James 1:13-17). It is the devil who comes into our lives to steal, kill, and destroy. God only comes to give us life, and to give us life abundantly (John 10:10). Everything that happens in life is not the result of God's will. Some things are just attacks from the devil. Thankfully, God has given us the authority to rebuke and resist those attacks. God's Word says,

> *Submit yourselves therefore to God. Resist the devil, and he will flee from you.*

> *James 4:7*

Any teaching that doesn't conform to the Word of God is false, no matter how popular it may be. You have to evaluate your philosophy and make sure it is based on the Word of God, and not

---

[6] *The American Heritage College Dictionary*, 3rd Edition, "stoic."

on the philosophies of this world or the traditions of men. Everything that God has shown me has helped to form my philosophy. It is all woven together into one dominant way of thinking. The Word of God has dictated my philosophy, and my response to life is, in turn, dictated by my philosophy. So the blessings in my life are simply a result of filtering life through God's perspective.

But Stoicism and Epicureanism aren't the only philosophies out there. The philosophy that your parents had when they raised you also has an impact on your belief system. Not merely their worldview, but the philosophy they instilled in you by the things they said, by the way they treated you, and through the behavior you witnessed.

I have a very close friend whose father was a good man in many ways, but he also had a mean streak. When my friend was a boy, his father used to browbeat him constantly. He was always scolding him for doing things incorrectly. Those negative statements became part of the way my friend looked at life. He saw himself as the man his father told him he was.

They lived on a farm, so the father was always fixing cars and other equipment and my friend would help. One of the things my friend's father used to tell him was that he couldn't put a nut on a bolt without crossing the threads. I remember working on a car with him one time and I watched him start to shake as he put a nut on a bolt. After he got the nut on, he was afraid it wasn't on right, so he kept taking it off and putting it back on until he actually cross threaded the bolt. The things his father spoke over him became a curse because my friend took those words to heart and made them a part of his philosophy.

All of us have been influenced by the philosophies we were raised with or that we picked up through experiences. Racism is an example of a philosophy that is handed down from one generation to the next; it's a kind of tradition. If a child raised in a racist environment doesn't replace those lies with the truth, he or she will incorporate prejudice into their worldview and it will affect their experience of life.

America had a tradition of racism that was hard to overcome. Martin Luther King, Jr. made a stand for morality and led our country through some difficult times. He didn't stick his head in the sand and hope that the problem of racism would go away. He stood up for a Christian philosophy that says all men are created equal, and he helped to change a nation. Today, society often fails to recognize that Martin Luther King, Jr. wasn't merely a civil rights leader, he was a Christian leader.

In the same way that society persecuted Martin Luther King, Jr. for his stand against racism, I can guarantee you that Christians are not going to be universally loved for making a stand against current wrongs in our society. Abortion is a heinous crime, but the majority of society supports it and there are elements that promote it aggressively. Still, we shouldn't be focused on how other people are going to respond. Our goal should be to do the will of God and to stand for what is right—that's a Christian philosophy.

Why Should I Care About Philosophy?

Righteousness exalteth a nation: but sin is a reproach to any people.

Proverbs 14:34

Righteousness is conforming your character and conduct to a right standard. It's conforming to the Word of God, not to philosophies of this world and the traditions of men. What the majority of society says is or is not right, is irrelevant. The majority is often wrong. The Word has to be the standard upon which we build our philosophy.

Too many Christians aren't building their philosophy on the Word. Some of them might not truly be born again, but some sincere Christians just haven't become disciples of the Lord Jesus. They haven't learned what the Word says, and they aren't following Him. They haven't made an effort to conform their heart and actions to a godly standard of righteousness. All they have done is accept Jesus to avoid going to hell. They often have philosophies that are completely contrary to the Word of God, but they don't see any problem with that. Obviously, if you have a philosophy that is contrary to the Word of God, you don't have a Christian philosophy.

Some of this is the fault of the church. We have been preaching salvation in order to go to heaven when we die, but we haven't been making disciples as the Lord commanded us. Some people are truly ignorant of God's values, but others are willfully ignorant. Those people are choosing not to subscribe to God's viewpoint because it doesn't fit with their lifestyle. Either way, ignorance isn't good for you. God loves you no matter what because He doesn't relate to us based on our performance, but ignorance isn't going to excuse you from the devil's attacks. The world's philosophy says that what you don't know won't hurt you, but the truth is that ignorance kills (Hosea 4:6).

You can see the influences of Epicurean philosophy in those who aim to please themselves no matter the consequences. The overwhelming majority of abortions are performed on women who aren't married. They are having sexual relations outside of marriage and using abortion as a form of birth control. God's command restricting sex to a marriage relationship is given to protect us emotionally, and to protect children. Sadly, 70% of women getting an abortion in the United States identify themselves as Christians at the time of the abortion.[7] This shows the degree to which men and women who have a philosophy putting pleasure first are doing what they want to and not worrying about the consequences— even when it means killing an unborn baby.

Christians should not be getting abortions. I'm not saying God is mad at you or that He won't love you anymore if you've ever had an abortion. God dealt with sin when He poured out His wrath on Jesus on the cross, and He isn't dealing with sin anymore. God is a good God who is full of mercy and unfailing love. So I'm not condemning women who have had an abortion. God's grace is more than enough to cover all of our sins. I'm simply saying that abortion is wrong. Abortion kills innocent children, and there is no room in a Christian philosophy for the tolerance of abortion.

---

[7] RK Jones, LB Finer, S Singh, *Characteristics of U.S. Abortion Patients, 2008,* (New York: Guttmacher Institute, 2010).

We can't just entertain the information that suits us. A ragbag collection of truths and half-truths will never add up to unified worldview that is godly and righteous. We need to get our philosophy from the Word of God. Filtering our lives through Scripture and basing our decisions on the philosophy that comes from the Word will keep us on the right path and prevent us from falling into hypocrisy. The reason there is such a wide variance in convictions among Christians is that not everyone is getting their philosophy from the Word.

Our citizenship in heaven can have more influence over us than our upbringing or the worldly ideas that surround us. As the apostle Paul said, "Let God be true, but every man a liar" (Romans 3:4). Even the religious instruction we received should be tossed aside if it doesn't conform to the Word of God. You might have been taught that God is angry and that He is just waiting to punish you the moment you step out of line, or that He uses sickness to correct people. Those are wrong doctrines, and they will allow the enemy to steal from you. Our beliefs need to be established upon what the Word says, not upon someone else's interpretation of it.

The Bible isn't just another book. It is a supernatural book through which God speaks to us. The Word of God is true. Once you get into the true Word of God and let the Holy Spirit instruct you, you'll see that it is the greatest revelation the world has ever been given. The Bible is a tremendous gift from God that contains the greatest philosophy known, and if you base your life upon the Word, you'll get supernatural results.

Chapter Three

Is the Bible True?

...for the Lord seeth not as man seeth; for man looketh on the outward appearance, but the Lord looketh on the heart.

1 Samuel 16:7

Although people focus on behavior and appearance, the Bible approaches change from the heart level. Humans want to deal with external things, but God's way is to deal with the heart. The heart is the source of your external behaviors; it's where your speech and actions come from (Luke 6:45). Men put emphasis on cleaning up the outward appearance, but God says clean the inside and the outside will be clean also (Matthew 23:26). If you want your external circumstances to change, you have to go to the heart and change your philosophy. The way you do that is by meditating on the Word. Religion consists of man's thoughts about God, but the Bible isn't a compilation of men's thoughts—it contains God's thoughts and His philosophy for us.

Satan has been pretty successful in robbing many Christians of the blessings that God has provided. The reason he has been so successful is that our philosophy is wrong. We have developed philosophies based on our upbringing and the ungodly influences of this world rather than on the Word of God. Satan comes to steal and to deprive us of what God has given by challenging the way we think. This is evident even from his first dealings with mankind. Concerning the dangers of wrong thinking, the apostle Paul said,

> *But I fear, lest by any means, as the serpent beguiled Eve through his subtlety, so your minds should be corrupted from the simplicity that is in Christ.*
>
> *2 Corinthians 11:3*

The way Satan came against Adam and Eve is the same way he comes against us today. The devil doesn't have any new tricks; he's still doing the same old thing. It's not like he has a million different ways of tempting people. His only method always boils down to lies and deception.

Temptation falls into just three basic categories: the lust of the flesh, the lust of the eyes, and the pride of life (1 John 2:16). Those are the areas in which Adam and Eve were tempted (Genesis 3:6), those are the areas in which Satan tried to tempt Jesus (Luke 4:1-12), and they are the same three areas in which the enemy is trying to tempt us today. You're being tempted in exactly the same ways that Adam and Eve were tempted. The devil just takes the same old stuff and repackages it, which is helpful in a way because we can avoid making the same mistakes Adam and Eve made by looking at the tactics Satan used against them.

The first thing we notice is that Satan is subtle. Scripture says, "Now the serpent was more subtle than any beast of the field which the LORD God had made" (Genesis 3:1). We know that Satan was behind using the serpent to lie because the Word says that Satan is the father of all lies (John 8:44). The devil created lying, and every time someone lies they are under the influence of the devil. So this serpent came and lied to Adam and Eve.

I already pointed out that Satan didn't use some huge animal to intimidate Eve and force her to eat the forbidden fruit. He didn't have any power whatsoever to force Adam and Eve into disobeying God. Instead, what he did was choose the most subtle animal—the most cunning, crafty, and sly creature. Why? Because it was a battle of wits. The battle against temptation has always been waged in the mind.

You'll sometimes hear people talk about "spiritual warfare" in the sense of going out and doing battle in the heavens. This is based in a misunderstanding of a verse that says we are battling evil powers in heavenly, or high, places (Ephesians 6:11-12). People have actually chartered planes so they could "take their prayers to the sky," or they have gone to the top of skyscrapers to do battle "in heaven." That isn't what this scripture is talking about. The battle against the enemy isn't somewhere out in the atmosphere; the battle is right between your ears.

Satan comes at you through your thoughts with lies and deception. It's the same way he has always operated, and that's the reason he chose the serpent to speak to Eve. It was the most cunning, crafty, and sly creature. It was able to twist and to deceive better than any other animal, so Satan motivated the snake to go and tempt Adam and Eve.

This is really significant. It shows how deception was Satan's only weapon. It demonstrates that he doesn't have the power to make people do anything. **Satan can't do anything without your consent and cooperation.** You have to reject his lies. Quit consenting to his deception, quit cooperating with him, and you'll leave him powerless. He won't be able to steal your health, your finances, or your peace of mind.

When Satan came against Adam and Eve through the serpent, the conversation started like this:

> *And he said unto the woman, Yea, hath God said, Ye shall not eat of every tree of the garden?*

> *Genesis 3:1*

Satan's primary method of attack is to challenge the Word of God. "Did He *really* say that?" Satan asks, "Are you sure He didn't mean something else?" Satan always challenges the Word, he always asks, "Is the Word really true?" The answer is YES! If Adam and Eve had responded, "Yes, God did say that, now get out of here"—that would have been the end of the story. There would have been no Fall, no sin, and suffering wouldn't have entered the world.

This reveals a fundamental principle of establishing a Christian philosophy, or a Christian way of thinking: Never forget that God's Word is always true. If you compromise on this point, Satan is going to rob you blind and nothing else is going to work. God's Word is the only sure foundation upon which to build a Christian philosophy.

Here's another tip. You can save yourself a lot of trouble by not even getting into conversations with the devil. When he attacks the Word, don't bother arguing with him, just state the truth and move on. But Eve didn't do that; she decided to have a chat with the serpent and said,

> *We may eat of the fruit of the trees of the garden: But of the fruit of the tree which is in the midst of the garden, God hath said, Ye shall not eat of it, neither shall ye touch it, lest ye die.*

> *Genesis 3:2-3*

The problem with what Eve said is that God never said they couldn't *touch* the fruit; He said don't *eat* it. Eve added to what God had said, and she thought that if she even touched the fruit she would die. When she was enticed by the lust of her eyes and flesh to reach out and touch the fruit and nothing happened, she thought maybe nothing would happen if she ate it too. She discovered that the thoughts she added to what God had said were false—she didn't die when she touched the fruit—and it tempted her to question all of what she believed about God's commands.

This same thing is happening today. Religion has added to the Word of God and nullified it in order to hand down traditions. This is exactly what Jesus accused the scribes and the Pharisees of doing (Mark 7:13). Religion is always adding rules and regulations to the Word of God. It is saying, "Don't even touch it or you'll die!"

Religion creates manmade traditions, and when people break the manmade traditions and don't die, they go ahead and break God's Word also, thinking that everything was just a hoax.

For example, some religious systems today are saying women shouldn't wear makeup or jewelry—which is a misunderstanding of the scripture that says women shouldn't be concerned with outward adorning, but rather be concerned with the beauty of their hearts. The scripture says don't be concerned with the "outward adorning of plaiting the hair, and of wearing of gold, or of putting on of apparel; But let it be the hidden man of the heart..." (1 Peter 3:3-4). If you interpret this to mean that there should be no plaiting of the hair or wearing of gold, then you have to say there shouldn't be any wearing of apparel either. Obviously, God doesn't want you running around without any clothes on. The intent of this scripture is to encourage people to focus on the condition of their hearts instead of their outward appearance.

Preaching that women should wear their hair in a certain way and dress a certain way or God won't love them anymore isn't true. When a young girl who has grown up hearing those things fails to live up to the supposed dress code but doesn't feel any different—because God *does* still love her—she calls into question everything she has ever learned about God. This is how religion and the traditions of men can nullify the Word of God.

Satan didn't come right out and say, "Hey, Adam and Eve, eat this forbidden fruit." No, he craftily attacked the Word by asking, "Did God *really* say...?" He cast doubt by criticizing what God had said. Similarly, Satan's biggest triumph in recent centuries has been to make it unfashionable to believe in and trust the Word of God. The world system, inspired by the devil, has come against the Word and put doubt in people's minds about its accuracy and relevance, so the majority of society is now off doing their own thing. But the doubt and uncertainty Satan has raised are all lies and deception.

Christians have to establish in their hearts that the Bible is the inspired Word of God. As I will show later, the Word is accurate, it is God-breathed, and it is God-inspired. If you ever start thinking the Bible is merely a book written by men *about* God, Satan is going to eat your lunch and pop the bag. You'll be in serious trouble if you ever adopt the mindset that the Bible has some truth in it, but it also has all kinds of error—leading you to go through and only pull out the parts that *you* think are relevant. If you do that, Satan will have you as surely as he had Adam and Eve.

I think the reason Satan tempted Eve instead of Adam was that Adam heard God's command directly. Genesis says, "And the LORD God commanded the man, saying, Of every tree of the garden thou mayest freely eat: But of the tree of the knowledge of good and evil, thou shalt not eat of it: for in the day that thou eatest thereof thou shalt surely die" (Genesis 2:16-17). The next verses describe how God decided Adam shouldn't be alone, so He created Eve to be a companion for Adam and instituted marriage between a man and a woman. So God gave the command not to eat the forbidden fruit before Eve was even formed, which means she might never have actually heard God give the command.

Any time you have one person repeating what someone else has told them, there is the possibility that they won't repeat it correctly. They might leave something out or add something that the first person never said. I remember playing a game like that as a kid. A bunch of people would line up in a row, and the first person would whisper a phrase to the next person in line. The message was passed down from person to person until you reached the end of the line, but each person only spoke the phrase once; you couldn't repeat it to make sure someone heard it correctly. By the time the last person in line spoke the phrase out loud, it wouldn't even resemble the original statement.

Similarly, Adam heard God in an audible voice tell him not to eat of the tree of the knowledge of good and evil, but Eve got her information secondhand from Adam. It would have been much harder for the serpent to convince Adam of what God did or didn't say because Adam heard God directly. So it was easier for the devil to make Eve doubt that Adam had repeated God's command accurately than it would have been to make Adam doubt what he had heard.

This story shows that we need to get our philosophy from God directly, and not depend upon other people to repeat it for us. You need to personalize the Word and make it real to you. It can't be just a book written to men in general, but not necessarily to you in particular. You have to believe the Bible is God's Word to *you*. The majority of people read the Bible like it's an interesting book about God, but they don't read it like it is God speaking to them. The Holy Spirit will use the words in the Bible to speak directly to you, and you have to read the Word with a sense of expectancy that God is going to speak to you through it.

I can't tell you how many people I have dealt with over the years who knew what God's Word says, but they were leaning on their own wisdom. They thought their opinion was better than God's, and they were doing things their own way. Some of those people had to crash and burn before they recognized that God was right, but you don't have to learn by the school of hard knocks. You can just believe the Word of God. The Bible says,

> *All scripture is given by inspiration of God, and is profitable for doctrine, for reproof, for correction, for instruction in righteousness: That the man of God may be perfect, thoroughly furnished unto all good works.*
>
> 2 Timothy 3:16-17

God has spoken to me through thousands of scriptures as I have prayed and asked Him for wisdom. He has used what is written in the Bible to speak directly to me. For instance, God has shown me how Moses' desire to accomplish God's plan in his own strength cost him forty years in the wilderness, and the nation of Israel spent an extra thirty years in bondage. Those things happened to Moses, but God has taken the scriptures and spoken them to me; He brought the words alive and gave me revelation knowledge that impacted my heart and shaped part of my Christian philosophy. The Bible is a book *from* God, He speaks to me through it, and I believe in the inspiration of Scripture with all of my heart.

God's Word will change you to the degree that you let it dominate your thoughts and life. I certainly haven't renewed my mind perfectly, but I'm also a long way from where I started. God's Word is working in my life. It has changed me, and I see the supernatural power of God as a result of believing what the Word says. God has been speaking to me through His Word for more than forty years—ever since He told me that the way to find His perfect will for my life was to make myself a living sacrifice and to renew my mind by conforming it to the truths in His Word (Romans 12:1-2).

The easiest way to prove to yourself that the Bible is God's Word and that He will speak to you through it, is just to read it. Begin by reading the entire New Testament. You might not understand everything the first time, but the Bible is its own commentary and the more you read, the more you will understand. Approach it with a sincere heart and say, "God, if this is really inspired by You and it isn't just the thoughts of men about You, then speak to me through it." If you pray in that way and remain open to the possibility that God will speak to you, I guarantee you will be inspired by God. The author of Hebrews wrote,

> *For the word of God is quick, and powerful, and sharper than any twoedged sword, piercing even to the dividing asunder of soul and spirit, and of the joints and marrow, and is a discerner of the thoughts and intents of the heart.*
>
> *Hebrews 4:12*

Is the Bible True?

The Word of God is alive, and it will come alive for you if you read it expectantly. Eve was the focus of Satan's temptation because God's command was secondhand to her. But we shouldn't be too hard on Eve for falling into temptation because she didn't really understand Satan or evil. She didn't know what was at stake. She didn't know what dying was, or what the effects of sin would be. In a sense, we can give her a pass because she was innocent and didn't realize what was happening when she succumbed to the lies of the devil.

But you and I don't get a pass. We live in a fallen world. We have all experienced failure, hurt, pain, and death. We understand the reality of evil. It doesn't make sense for us to bury our head in the sand and say, "Well, you know, I'm just not sure God speaks to me through the Bible. I'm not sure I can really trust this." You need to come to the resolution that God's Word is alive, and that He speaks to you personally through it. You can't get your knowledge secondhand from me or another preacher. You need to go to the Word and hear God speak to you directly, and then you'll have enough firsthand knowledge to be safe from the deception of false doctrines, traditions of men, and wrong philosophies.

Some Christians are relying on bits and pieces of Scripture that they heard decades ago as children in Sunday school. They are relying on the pastor of their church or another teacher to tell them what the Word says, but they aren't reading it for themselves. Those people are prime targets for the devil. The devil goes about like a roaring lion seeking people to devour, and just like a lion, he looks for the weak (1 Peter 5:8). He looks for people who don't have the armor and protection of knowing God's Word. This is one reason it is so important to know what God's Word says firsthand.

I'm not saying you can't learn from other people, but it shouldn't be the foundation of your relationship with God. A baby begins by being dependent upon his mother to feed him, but he doesn't stay that way. A baby can't grow up to be a fully function-ing adult if he stays dependent upon other people to feed him. In the same way, all Christians need to learn how to feed themselves from the Word of God. You can't remain dependent upon your pastor to feed you revelation. I know that the cares of this life keep people busy, but if you understand how vital it is to study the Word, you'll find the time to do it.

When the apostle Peter was getting toward the end of his life, he wrote a letter to believers in which he stressed the inspiration of Scripture and the confidence we can have that God is speaking to us through it. Peter knew that he was going to die shortly, and he was giving final encouragement to the believers. He said,

> *For we have not followed cunningly devised fables, when we made known unto you the power and coming of our Lord Jesus Christ, but were eyewitnesses of his majesty. For he received from God the Father honour and glory, when there came such a voice to him from the excellent glory, This is my beloved Son, in whom I am well pleased. And this voice which came from heaven we heard, when we were with him in the holy mount.*
>
> *2 Peter 1:16–18*

Peter was saying, "I'm about to die, but I'm going to write these things down so you can always have this to remember." He was making known that the account he gave of Jesus wasn't something he devised on his own. He wasn't just telling stories. The words he had written down were inspired by God, and they told of Peter's experiences. Peter was with Jesus on the Mount of Transfiguration and heard the audible voice of God say, "This is my beloved Son, in whom I am well pleased." He saw Jesus radiate light that no earthly power could produce. Peter was there! But then Peter writes,

> *We have also a more sure word of prophecy; whereunto ye do well that ye take heed, as unto a light that shineth in a dark place, until the day dawn, and the day star arise in your hearts: Knowing this first, that no prophecy of the scripture is of any private interpretation. For the prophecy came not in old time by the will of man: but holy men of God spake as they were moved by the Holy Ghost.*
>
> *2 Peter 1:19-21*

Peter saw Moses and Elijah talk with Jesus on the Mount of Transfiguration. He saw Jesus radiate light, and he heard God speak with an audible voice from heaven and confirm that Jesus was His Son, but he says we have something even better than that—better than seeing with our eyes or hearing with our ears—we have the written Word of God!

Most people would rather see what Peter saw and hear what he heard than read the Bible. Large crowds will turn out to hear you speak if you advertise that you had a vision and heard the voice of God. People come in droves to hear that sort of thing, but far fewer people show up when you advertise that you're going to be sharing what Scripture says. The reason is that our culture puts more emphasis on what we can perceive with our senses than on the Word of God. Peter said we should be doing just the opposite.

Peter clearly states that the Word of God was not written by men—it was not of "any private interpretation." The Holy Spirit inspired men to write the scriptures. The apostle Paul made the same point in his letter to Timothy when he said,

All scripture is given by inspiration of God, and is profitable for doctrine, for reproof, for correction, for instruction in righteousness: That the man of God may be perfect, thoroughly furnished unto all good works.

2 Timothy 3:16-17

The Greek word for "given by inspiration of God" is literally translated "divinely breathed."[8] This clearly states that the Word of God didn't come from the thoughts of men. God breathed His thoughts into men, who then put them in writing. The Bible is not a human book; it's God's book written for men.

I believe Scripture, and I've studied it enough to verify for myself that it is the Word of God. I don't need any further proof, but plenty of scholars have also authenticated the Bible from a historical and scientific view. Many books have been written about

[8] James Strong, *The New Strong's Expanded Exhaustive Concordance of the Bible* (Nashville: Nelson Publishers, 2001), 114. G2315, *theopneustos.*

the accuracy and inspiration of the Bible. I can't cover all of the evidence here, but I want to share a few facts that will give you confidence in the accuracy and inspiration of Scripture.

To begin with, the manuscript evidence supporting the New Testament far outstrips any evidence for secular writings of ancient times. One researcher has said, "The New Testament documents have more manuscripts, earlier manuscripts, and more abundantly supported manuscripts than the best ten pieces of classical literature *combined*."[9]

For example, *Caesar's Gallic War* was written between 58 and 50 BC. Ten copies of that original work remain, and the earliest was written 900 years after Caesar's day. Livy wrote a 142 volume *Roman History* sometime between 59 BC and 17 AD, but only 35 volumes survived, in not more than 20 different manuscripts. The text of Tacitus' 14 volume *Histories* and 16 volume *Annals* survives in only two manuscripts written 900 and 1,100 years *after* the original works. The earliest manuscripts of renowned Greek historians Thucydides and Herodotus that are complete enough to be of use to scholars were written more than 1,300 years after the originals.[10]

Homer's *Iliad* is the secular work that has the most supporting evidence, with 643 surviving copies (the earliest being written around 500 years after the original), but it doesn't even compare to the New Testament evidence we have. The number of differences between the copies of the *Iliad* is also greater—even though there

[9] Norman Geisler and Frank Turek, *I Don't Have Enough Faith to Be an Atheist* (Wheaton: Crossway Books, 2004), 225
[10] F.F. Bruce, *The New Testament Documents: Are they reliable?* 5th ed. rev. (Grand Rapids: The Inter-Varsity Press, 1988), 16.

are more than 20 times as many New Testament manuscripts being studied and compared.

In contrast to the copies of secular histories given above, *more than 5,600 Greek manuscripts of the New Testament have survived in whole or in part.* Those manuscripts vary in age, the more complete having been written within 150 years of the original, with the earliest manuscript portion written within 30 years of the original. (Keep in mind that the New Testament wasn't written as a single book, but is composed of many letters written by multiple authors at different times.) The fact that so many copies of the New Testament scriptures have survived, combined with the fact that they were written so closely to the originals, firmly establishes the historical accuracy of the scriptures we have today.

From a purely human perspective, the chance for error is increased when a document is copied over and over again thousands of times. The more times something is copied, the more errors you should see. This is true in the case of secular works, but not with the Bible. The abundance of ancient New Testament manuscripts have been compared and there are very few differences—and they contain no differences whatsoever that contradict the Gospel message of Jesus or the historical facts of Christian faith.[11] *Scholars have placed the comparative accuracy between the more than 5,600 manuscripts at 99.5%!*[12] This is astounding, and it shows how God has supernaturally preserved the integrity of the Bible through time.

---

[11] Bruce, New Testament, 20.
[12] Norman Geisler, *Baker Encyclopedia of Christian Apologetics* (Grand Rapids: Baker Books, 1998), 532.

Work	Time Written	Earliest Copies	Time Span between original and copy[13]	Number of Copies
Plato	427-347 BC	900 AD	1,200 years	7
Thucydides	460-400 BC	900 AD	1,300 years	8
Herodotus	488-428 BC	900 AD	1,300 years	8
Caesar	58-50 BC	900 AD	900 years	10
Livy	59 BC – 17 AD	?	?	20
Tacitus	100 AD	1,100 AD	1,000	20
Aristotle	384-322 BC	1100 AD	1,400 years	49
Homer (*Iliad*)	900 BC	400 BC	500 years	643
Greek copies of the New Testament	50-100 AD	300 AD and earlier	150[14]	5,686

The nearer in time to the original writing a copy is made, the more likely, in a purely natural sense, the work is to be correct. Also, the greater number of copies in existence, the easier it is to compare for accuracy. (It should be noted that, in addition to the Greek copies of the New Testament, there are thousands more copies of New Testament books which were produced in other

---

[13] The information in this chart is from: Bruce, New Testament, 16-20; Geisler, Baker Encyclopedia, 527-538; and The Christian Apologetics and Research Ministry online at http://carm.org/manuscript-evidence

[14] One small fragment of papyrus that has been discovered, known as the John Rylands papyri, was written only 30 years after the original Gospel of John.

languages during the same time frame. In fact, researchers have discovered more than 9,000 copies of New Testament manuscripts in other languages—bringing the total number of manuscripts to well over 14,000.) The abundance of ancient manuscripts and the nearness of their composition to the actual events, makes the New Testament the most verifiable document of antiquity.

Not only do we have copies of the scriptures themselves, but leaders in the early Christian church (often called the Church Fathers) wrote prolifically between 90 and 160 A.D. Their familiarity with the New Testament scriptures we still read today is proven by the fact that *all but 11 verses from the New Testament are quoted in their writings!*[15]

Non-Christians have also given evidence of Jesus as a historical figure in their writings. In 93 A.D., the Jewish historian Flavius Josephus wrote, "Now there was about this time Jesus, a wise man, if it be lawful to call him a man; for he was a doer of wonderful works, a teacher of such men as receive the truth with pleasure. He drew over to him both many of the Jews and many of the Gentiles. He was [the] Christ. And when Pilate, at the suggestion of the principal men amongst us, had condemned him to the cross, those that loved him at the first did not forsake him; for he appeared to them alive again the third day; as the divine prophets had foretold these and ten thousand other wonderful things concerning him. And the tribe of Christians, so named from him, are not extinct at this day."[16]

---

[15] Geisler, Enough Faith, 229.

[16] Flavius Josephus, *The Works of Flavius Josephus*, trans. William Whiston (Buffalo: John E. Beardsley, 1895), 18.3.3 online at www.perseus.tufts.edu

Josephus also wrote about the persecution and death of James. He said that the Sanhedrin "...brought before them the brother of Jesus, who was called Christ, whose name was James, and some others, [or, some of his companions]; and when he had formed an accusation against them as breakers of the law, he delivered them to be stoned."[17]

The Roman historian Tacitus described how the emperor Nero set fire to Rome, and in an effort to deflect the wrath of its citizens, he blamed the fire on the Christians. Tacitus said:

"Nero fastened the guilt and inflicted the most exquisite tortures on a class hated for their abominations, called Christians by the populace. Christus, from whom the name had its origin, suffered the extreme penalty during the reign of Tiberius at the hands of one of our procurators, Pontius Pilatus, and a most mischievous superstition, thus checked for the moment, again broke out not only in Judæa, the first source of the evil, but even in Rome, where all things hideous and shameful from every part of the world find their centre and become popular. Accordingly, an arrest was first made of all who pleaded guilty; then, upon their information, an immense multitude was convicted, not so much of the crime of firing the city, as of hatred against mankind. Mockery of every sort was added to their deaths. Covered with the skins of beasts, they were torn by dogs and perished, or were nailed to crosses, or were doomed to the flames and burnt, to serve as a nightly illumination, when daylight had expired."[18]

[17] Josephus, Works of, 20.9.1.
[18] Cornelius Tacitus, *Complete Works of Tacitus*, ed. Alfred John Church et. al. (New York: Perseus, Random House, 1942), 15.44 online at www. perseus.tufts.edu

Without taking into account the evidence contained in the New Testament, we can still show from non-Christian writers that Jesus was a historical figure who lived in Palestine in the early years of the first century, that He gathered followers, and that He was crucified under Pontius Pilate.[19] In fact, within 150 years of Jesus' life, ten non-Christian writers mentioned Jesus. Over that same time span, only nine mention the Roman emperor who ruled during Jesus' life—Tiberius Caesar. Not even considering Christian authors, Jesus is more documented than the Roman emperor![20] It is undeniable that Jesus was a man who lived and walked the earth precisely when Scripture says He did.

The discovery of the Dead Sea Scrolls between 1946 and 1957 in several caves on the shores of the Dead Sea has given us further evidence of the accuracy of the Scriptures that have been handed down to us. Among the Dead Sea Scrolls was an intact copy of the entire book of Isaiah (known as the Great Isaiah Scroll). It is dated at 100 B.C. and is 1000 years older than the copies that were used to compose the book of Isaiah we read in our Bibles today. After 1,000 years of being copied and recopied by hand, the number of differences between the Great Isaiah Scroll and our book of Isaiah is miniscule, with the variations consisting mostly of spelling mistakes and simple copying errors.[21] The discovery of the Dead Sea Scrolls also proves that the Messianic prophecies we read in Isaiah

---

[19] Bruce M. Metzger, *The New Testament: its background, growth, and content*, 15th ed. (Nashville: Abingdon Press, 1980), 78.
[20] Geisler, Enough Faith, 222.
[21] Geisler, Baker Encyclopedia, 187-189.

were definitely written prior to the birth of Jesus, which reinforces the case that Scripture makes for Jesus as the Messiah.

The bottom line is that the Bible has been handed down through the ages with such accuracy that it can't be just a human book. The different copies we have of ancient secular writings have significant differences in them because they were simply copied by men—they weren't inspired and preserved by God. The Bible, on the other hand, has been supernaturally preserved by God and all of the evidence we have supports that it was written by the inspiration of God. The last words of David, king of Israel and author of the Messianic prophecies in Psalm 22, reveal how the Holy Spirit inspired the men who wrote Scripture:

> *The Spirit of the LORD spake by me, and his word was in my tongue.*
>
> *2 Samuel 23:2*

"We still can't trust the Bible," some will argue, "because it's only a translation, and translations aren't inspired." Well, Jesus didn't share that opinion. Jesus quoted from the Septuagint, which was a Greek translation of the Hebrew Old Testament, and He equated Scripture with words proceeding from the mouth of God (Matthew 4:4). Jesus' use of Scripture throughout the Gospels also shows that He believed it was the final authority; particularly when the devil was challenging God's commands.

Additionally, the apostle Paul hinged the thrust of his letter to the Galatians on the fact that God made His promise to the seed (singular) of Abraham, instead of to his seeds (plural) (Galatians

3:16). Paul made an argument for Jesus as the promised seed of Abraham based on the singular form of one word from a translation of the original Old Testament scripture—which shows that God is well able to preserve the truth in His Word for us, even through translations.

I spend nearly all of my time studying the Word. Scripture says, "Thy word have I hid in mine heart, that I might not sin against thee" (Psalm 119:11). We're not told to hide historical information about New Testament manuscripts in our hearts. Nevertheless, scholarship and historical inquiry *do* support the claims of Christianity; ancient manuscript discoveries show that the Scriptures we read today are the same as the original inspired writings, and further research shows that the New Testament is completely unique among the books of antiquity. No other book in history is as verifiable as the Bible—which is exactly what you would expect from a book given to us by God.

But even if there was no evidence outside the Bible that the Word of God is inspired, I would still be fully convinced. I don't have enough space to tell you every way that the Word of God has been proven true in my life. It has shown me how to deal with sickness, problems, and rejection. The Word showed me how to find a wife, and how to stay married after I found her! I couldn't tell you how many times I have applied the truths from God's Word in my life and watched God's promises come to pass. I have verified for myself beyond all doubt that Scripture is the inspired Word of God, and it is accurate in all of its detail.

Is the Bible True?

People sometimes don't understand how the Bible can say things in different books that seem to be in opposition to one another. Atheists love to pick out scriptures meant to balance one another and pretend that the statements are mutually exclusive, and therefore—they say—the Bible is flawed and can't be from God. But that isn't true. Certain passages in the Bible might appear to be contradictions, but opposite statements are sometimes intentional. The Bible is its own commentary, and separate—apparently opposing—scriptures can hold a single truth in balance by presenting it in different ways.

For example, one scripture says "For by grace are ye saved through faith; and that not of yourselves: it is the gift of God: Not of works, lest any man should boast" (Ephesians 2:8-9). Another says, "But wilt thou know, O vain man, that faith without works is dead?" (James 2:20). Both statements are true, and each is a commentary on the other; they describe the balance of grace and faith.

Every Christian needs to come to the conclusion that the Word of God is accurate and inspired. The Word has to be the foundation of your worldview, or Satan is going to steal from you. The devil is roaming about looking to devour people who doubt God's Word—just as he was able to spoil Eve because she wasn't absolutely convinced that God's command was true. The Word of God is 100% trustworthy. Personally, I doubt my little peanut brain before I question the accuracy of the Word. I haven't figured everything out, but I know the problem isn't with the Word—it's with my inability to interpret and comprehend the depths of God.

Accepting God's Word as being absolute truth and authority goes against cultural norms today. In most Western nations, the majority of people who say they believe the Bible is God's Word do not seem to believe that it is accurate and trustworthy enough to base their lives upon it. The majority of believers are getting their philosophy elsewhere, and that's why their worldview doesn't line up with God's perspective.

You will not prosper in the Lord unless you accept the Bible as God's Word. You may have periods in your life where it looks like you are doing fine, but deviating from the Word of God leads to wrong ways of thinking and, eventually, those wrong thought patterns are going to cause you trouble. Eve was fine for a while too—until she began to question God's Word, and then Satan gained a foothold into her life and plunged the entire human race into the destruction we see today.

The best thing you can do for yourself and for your relationship with God is trust that His Word is inspired and accurate in all of its detail. If the Word of God says something is okay, then it's okay. And when His Word says something is wrong, then it's wrong. Basing your worldview on the Bible will lead you to respond to life in a positive way and put you on the path to prosperity. It will also prevent the devil from gaining access to you through wrong philosophies, the traditions of men, or the wisdom and principles of this world. The Word of God is the only sure foundation to build your philosophy on, and it is your ticket to the blessed life.

Chapter Four

How Do We Know the Bible Is Inspired?

Instead of looking to God for guidance, many Christians today are turning to science or the principles of this world to answer their questions—but that is exactly what the apostle Paul warned not to do (Colossians 2:8). The Word of God is a far more reliable place to look for answers, and a much more sure foundation for our worldview. Jesus didn't go around citing the traditions of the Pharisees or the laws of the scribes; He quoted the Word of God as the final authority.

Science itself is not bad; it is merely the observation and interpretation of data. The problem lies in the interpretation, which is sometimes based on the assumption that God doesn't exist—an obvious problem for Christians. Unfortunately, many people today have chosen to put their faith in science, which really means they are putting their faith in the interpretations and opinions of men rather than God. However, despite efforts by atheists to disprove the existence of God, not a single scrap of scientific evidence has ever been produced that invalidates Scripture.

The word "science" is used by many to imply "incontrovertible laws," but nothing could be further from the truth. Throughout history, what was promoted as being unassailably true by science one day has often been disproven the next. Scientific theories are in a constant state of revision. The principles of this world are here today and gone tomorrow, but the Bible has stood the test of time. The Word of God remains unchanged. Jesus said,

> *Heaven and earth shall pass away, but my words shall not pass away.*

> *Matthew 24:35*

The Bible is not a science textbook, nor does it attempt to answer questions of mathematics and natural science, but the Bible has always proven accurate in all of its prophecies and details. This is remarkable when you consider that Scripture was written during a time when the world was steeped in superstition and ignorance. This once again underscores the fact that the Bible was written by God, through men.

For instance, the Bible teaches that the universe had a beginning (Genesis 1:1), when the common ancient view was that the universe was eternal. Isaiah wrote that the earth was round in 800 BC (Isaiah 40:22), but Western society didn't embrace that truth for another two thousand years. The Word teaches that no new matter is being created in the universe (Genesis 2:2), and the first law of thermodynamics states the same thing. The second law of thermodynamics claims that the amount of energy in the universe is decreasing, which is what the Psalmist declared:

How Do We Know the Bible Is Inspired?

Of old hast thou laid the foundation of the earth: and the
heavens are the work of thy hands. They shall perish, but thou
shalt endure: yea, all of them shall wax old like a garment; as a
vesture shalt thou change them, and they shall be changed: But
thou art the same, and thy years shall have no end.

Psalm 102:25-27

I don't base my faith in God on the ability of scholars to reconcile the Word of God to current scientific theories, and I don't
believe we should, because the Bible is more trustworthy than the
fashionable ideas of any time period. God is unchanging, and His
Word has proven true over and over again. However, the scientific
accuracy contained in the Bible—which was written well ahead of
any contemporary discovery—is another indication of its supernatural origins.

Even more than any external evidence, I think that Scripture
itself is the greatest proof that the Word of God is accurate and
inspired. Back when I first started walking with God, before I
had proven the Word true in my life, the one thing that really
convinced me of the inspiration of the Bible was the amount of
prophecy in Scripture that has been fulfilled and the accuracy of
those prophecies. Mere human predictions are usually so vague
that they can be fulfilled in a hundred different ways. A horoscope
in the newspaper or a fortune cookie from a restaurant can do that.
The prophecies of the Bible are on a whole different level. The
Bible is in a category all by itself.

The Old Testament prophecies about the Messiah were written four hundred years or more before New Testament times, and Jesus fulfilled them down to every last detail. The total number of prophecies Jesus fulfilled is in the hundreds, but I'll just mention a few of them here.[22]

It was prophesied in Scripture that the Messiah would not see corruption (meaning that His body wouldn't decay—Psalm 16:9-10), which was fulfilled when Jesus rose from the dead (Acts 2:27, 31; 13:35). Scripture says that Christ would feel forsaken (Psalm 22:1), and when Jesus was on the cross He called out "My God, my God, why hast thou forsaken me?" (Matthew 27:46; Mark 15:34). It says that the Messiah would be mocked and ridiculed (Psalm 22:7-8), and that came to pass exactly (Luke 23:35).

It says they would pierce His hands and His feet (Psalm 22:16). You can't get any more specific than that—and at the time this prophecy was written, the Roman's hadn't even invented the punishment of crucifixion yet! Yet Scripture describes Jesus' crucifixion perfectly (Mark 15:25; Luke 23:33; John 19:37; 20:25).

Scripture prophesied that people would divide Jesus' garments and cast lots for them (Psalm 22:18). The soldiers at the cross did precisely that (Luke 23:34; John 19:23-24). They divided His clothes among themselves, and when they got to His robe, they discovered it was an expensive robe woven as one piece without a single seam. Rather than tear it apart, they cast lots for it.

---

[22] Andrew Wommack, Living Commentary Bible software, note for Matthew 26:24.

Scripture prophesied that not one of Jesus' bones would be broken (Psalm 34:20). The Romans often broke the leg bones of those being crucified to hasten death, but when they came to Jesus they saw He was already dead, so they didn't break His bones (John 19:36).

Scripture prophesied that Jesus would be hated without cause (Psalm 35:19), and be betrayed by a close friend (Psalm 41:9). The Word says that He would be despised and rejected by men (Isaiah 53:3); people passing by would wag their heads at Him (Psalm 109:25); He would be given vinegar mixed with gall to drink (Psalm 69:21); He would die but rise from the dead, and He would ascend to the right hand of God. All of those prophecies were fulfilled (Matthew 27:34, 39; Luke 22:47-48; John 1:10-11;15:24-25).

It says the Messiah would bear our sicknesses and carry our diseases (Isaiah 53:4-5). Jesus' life demonstrated God's desire to heal us, and many scriptures confirm that Jesus purchased health for us in His atonement (Matthew 8:16-17; 1 Peter 2:24). The Word prophesied that Christ would cause the deaf to hear, the blind to see, the dumb to talk, and the lame to leap (Isaiah 35:4-6). The entire New Testament is a record of "How God anointed Jesus of Nazareth with the Holy Ghost and with power: who went about doing good, and healing all that were oppressed of the devil; for God was with him" (Acts 10:38). And He's still doing it. The Holy Spirit is continuing Jesus' earthly ministry by giving sight to the blind, health to the sick, and liberty to captives (Luke 4:17-18).

Scripture says Jesus was wounded for our transgressions (Isaiah 53:5). It prophesied He would stay silent before His accusers (Isaiah 53:7), which is completely contrary to human nature. An innocent person facing a severely painful and cruel death would try to make some kind of a defense to get out of it, but Jesus didn't say a word (Matthew 27:12, 14; Mark 14:61; 15:5; 1 Peter 2:23).

Scripture prophesied that the Messiah would be killed with sinners and buried with the rich (Isaiah 53:9, 12). Jesus was crucified between two thieves (Mark 15:27-28) and buried in a rich man's tomb (Matthew 27:57-60). Like the virgin birth, being born in Bethlehem, or the manner of His death, these are prophecies that no man can control through his own effort.

Old Testament Scripture	Some Prophecies Regarding the Messiah that Were Fulfilled in Jesus	New Testament Fulfillment
Ps. 16:10	He would not see corruption	Acts 2:27-31
Ps. 22:1	He would feel forsaken	Matt. 27:46; Mark 15:34
Ps. 22:7-8	He would be mocked and ridiculed	Matt. 27:29; Mark 15:19-20; Luke 23:35
Ps. 22:16	His hands and feet would be pierced	Mark 15:25; Luke 23:33
Ps. 22:18	They would cast lots for His clothing	Matt. 27:35; Mark 15:24; Luke 23:34; John 19:24
Ps. 34:20	None of the Messiah's bones would be broken	John 19:31-36
Ps. 35:11	He would be falsely accused	Mark 14:57-58

Ps. 35:19	He would be hated without cause	John 15:24-25
Ps. 41:9	He would be betrayed by a close friend	Luke 22:47-48
Ps. 69:21	He would be given vinegar mixed with gall to drink	Matt. 27:34; 48; Mark 15:36; John 19:29
Ps. 109:25	Those who looked upon Him would wag their heads	Matt. 27:39
Ps. 49:15; 16:10	He would conquer death by resurrection	Acts 2:24-36; Mark 16:6-7
Ps. 68:18	His ascension to the right hand of God	Mark 16:19; Acts 1:9-10; Eph. 4:8
Mic. 5:2-5	Be born in the town of Bethlehem in Judea	Matt. 2:1-6
Is. 7:14	He would be born of a virgin	Matt. 1:18-23; Luke 1:26-35
Is. 35:4-6; 29:18	He would cause the deaf to hear, the blind to see, the dumb to talk, and the lame to leap	Matt. 11:5; 15:30; 21:14; John 5:8-9; Acts 3:2-8
Is. 52:14	Others would mar His appearance, and He would be so disfigured that He hardly looked human	Matt. 26:67; 27:26; 29-30; Mark 15:15-19; John 19:34
Is. 53:3	He would be despised and rejected of men	John 1:10-11
Is. 53:4-5	He would bear our sickness and carry our diseases	Matt. 8:16-17; 1 Pet. 2:24
Is. 53:5-6	He was wounded for our transgressions ("offences")	Rom. 4:25; 1 Pet. 3:18

Is. 53:7	He would be silent before His accusers, as a lamb led to the slaughter	Matt. 27:12-14; Mark 14:61; 15:5; 1 Pet. 2:23
Is. 53:9	He would be buried with the rich	Matt. 27:57-60
Is. 53:11	His death would justify many	Rom. 5:18-19; 1 John 2:1-2
Is. 53:12	He would be numbered with transgressors in His death	Matt. 27:38; Mark 15:28; Luke 22:37
Zech. 9:9	He would come to Jerusalem riding on a donkey	Mark 11:1-10; Matt. 21:1-5; Luke 19:28-38; John 12:12-15
Zech. 11:12-13	He would be betrayed for thirty pieces of silver, and it would be used to buy a potter's field	Matt. 27:3-10

One mathematician famously calculated the probability of just eight of these Old Testament prophecies being fulfilled accidentally as one in one hundred quadrillion, or 10^{17}—a number beyond comprehension.[23] In other words, the odds that the following things could have happened by chance is 1 in 100 quadrillion: A man who was born in Bethlehem would have a prophet go before him and prepare his way, that he would be a ruler who entered Jerusalem on a donkey, be betrayed by a friend and that betrayal would result in wounding his hands; that he would be betrayed for exactly 30 pieces of silver, and those 30 pieces of silver would later be thrown on the Temple floor and used to buy a potter's field; when on trial for his life—though innocent—he would make no

---

[23] Peter Stoner, *Science Speaks* (Chicago: Moody Press, 1976) online at http://sciencespeaks.dstoner.net/Christ_of_Prophecy.html#c9

defense, and he would be one of the few men in all of history who was killed by crucifixion. The odds of all of that happening to any man are 1 in 10^{17}.

To give you a sense of how large a number one hundred quadrillion is, consider this: if you had 100 quadrillion dollars, and you spent 1 million dollars every *second* of every day, it would take you 3,168 years to spend all of that money.

Or, if you stacked $1 dollar bills on top of each other, 100 quadrillion dollars would make 73 separate stacks of bills stretching the 93 million miles from earth to the sun (pretending that the heat of the sun didn't incinerate the paper bills). Let's say that somewhere in those 73 stacks is a single dollar bill marked with a black "X". Imagine a ladder that leans up against those stacks of bills and stretches all the way to the sun. Now, get on that ladder and start climbing. Stop anywhere you want along the *93 million miles* and pull a single bill from any one of the 73 stacks. The chances that you will pick the one dollar bill with a black "X" on it are the same chances that any man could have accidentally fulfilled eight of the prophecies that Jesus fulfilled as the Messiah.

One hundred quadrillion is an *absurdly* large number. When you consider that Jesus fulfilled hundreds of prophecies—not a mere eight—you begin to understand what a testimony to the inspiration of Scripture Jesus' life truly was (in addition to certain proof that He is the Messiah).

Other prophecies in the Bible predicted events unrelated to the Messiah that were also fulfilled historically. For instance, about two hundred years before Cyrus, king of Persia, was born, the prophet Isaiah said that God would raise up a Gentile king named Cyrus who would facilitate the rebuilding of the Temple (Isaiah 44:28)—and that is exactly what happened (2 Chronicles 36:22).

Another prophecy arose when Jeroboam, king of Israel, was offering sacrifices to a demon god and a prophet stood before the altar and cried, "O altar, altar, thus saith the LORD; Behold, a child shall be born unto the house of David, Josiah by name; and upon thee shall he offer the priests of the high places that burn incense upon thee, and men's bones shall be burnt upon thee" (1 Kings 13:2). About three hundred years later, the prophecy was fulfilled by the righteous king Josiah (2 Kings 23:15-20).

By the time Josiah was born, the nation of Israel had fallen far from God. The ten northern tribes in Israel had already been led into captivity by Gentiles, but the southern tribes of Judah and Benjamin where still in existence. Josiah was king over both tribes, but he only learned how far they had strayed from God after a copy of the book of the Law was found in the Temple—most likely a copy of the Pentateuch (the first five books of the Bible), written by Moses (2 Kings 22:8). After reading the Old Testament scriptures, Josiah became convicted about the condition of the kingdom and set out to restore righteousness. He put a stop to pagan worship and then he dug up the graves of the false prophets and burned their bones on the very altar on which Jeroboam had sacrificed to idols. You can't get any more specific than that.

How Do We Know the Bible Is Inspired?

No book written by a human has prophesied events hundreds of years in advance down to every last detail. The supposed prophecies of people like Nostradamus are so vague that they can be fulfilled in a multitude of ways. In contrast, the Word of God describes in precise detail events that are then fulfilled hundreds of years later. The difference is that the Bible is inspired by God. It wasn't created by the minds of mere humans.

Christians who aren't basing their philosophy on the Word of God need to "rediscover" Scripture much like Josiah did. The Bible was written by men but inspired by God, and it contains God's thoughts for us. It shows us how God looks at the world, and everything we need to know about current social issues is in the Bible. It tells us God's perspective on murder, lying, stealing, homosexuality, divorce, integrity, abortion, and every other issue. The Bible is God's philosophy written out for us to understand.

Many Christians today are basically ignoring God's way of thinking and coming up with their own way of looking at things. They are trying a little of this and a little of that, and doing whatever works for them. I'm telling you, that is a recipe for disaster. Satan comes against us through the way we think. You give the enemy free access to your life when you base your philosophy on the world's viewpoint. The Word of God needs to become the standard you use to judge everything. Joshua said,

> *This book of the law shall not depart out of thy mouth; but thou shalt meditate therein day and night, that thou mayest observe to do according to all that is written therein: for then*

thou shalt make thy way prosperous, and then thou shalt have good success.

Joshua 1:8

You aren't going to prosper and succeed until you take the Word of God and put it in your heart and meditate on it. Some people in the world appear to be prospering, they have power and possessions, but those things don't last. You can prosper momentarily outside of pursuing God, but that kind of prosperity isn't going to fulfill you. Tabloids are filled with stories of the rich and famous trying to commit suicide. Many wealthy and powerful people who don't know God are more miserable and bitter than the poorest of the poor. Jesus said, "For what is a man profited, if he shall gain the whole world, and lose his own soul? Or what shall a man give in exchange for his soul?" (Matthew 16:26).

There is a right and a wrong way to prosper. If you want to prosper God's way, in a way that doesn't take away your life, then you're going to have to base your prosperity on the Word of God. You have to take God's values and do things God's way.

When you do things God's way, life isn't all about acquiring possessions—it's about relationship with God and experiencing His love. Scripture tells us that if we seek God's kingdom first, then He will give us everything we need (Matthew 6:33). God will take care of you when you are seeking Him first. The Word contains God's instructions to us on how to prosper. It gives His revelation on how to make your marriage work, how to walk in health, and how to have joy and peace.

The evidence we have examined leaves no doubt that the Bible is the inspired Word of God. The Bible contains God's instructions for our success, and it is accurate in every detail. We have to put our faith in the Word of God, above all other information or ideas. If you compromise on this point or begin to doubt that the Bible is the inspired Word of God, then you start down a slippery slope that will undermine your faith in God. The Bible is not a book about God, it is a book *from* God, and it has to be the foundation of all Christian philosophy.

Chapter Five

How Do I Follow God?

I remember a young man who came to me for counsel one time about going to Charis Bible College. He said that he knew God was telling him to go, but everyone in his life was telling him not to. He went into a long story detailing all of the reasons the pastor of his church, his parents, and his girlfriend thought he shouldn't go.

After about ten minutes he finally asked me, "So what do you think?"

I said, "You lost me the moment you said that you know God is telling you to go."

If God tells you to do something, then you just do what God tells you to do. Why would you even debate it? God is the Creator of the universe, He knows all things, and He knows what is best for you. Why would you care what anybody else thinks, or what people might say about you? In comparison with God, no one else's opinion should matter.

Your relationship with God should soak all the way down to the very core of your being. When that happens, your actions will be determined by your philosophy instead of by your environment or emotions. It really simplifies life to realize Jesus is Lord, and you aren't. Then, when God tells you to do something, you just do it. This attitude is one part of a Christian philosophy that will really simplify your life.

I couldn't tell you how many people have told me over the years that they felt God was calling them to come to Charis Bible College, but they didn't think it was wise to go. They've said, for instance, that it's only ten years until they retire. They were focused on securing their financial future, and they were leaning unto their own understanding. My opinion is that when God wants you to do something ten years from now, He'll tell you ten years from now. If God is telling you now, He either wants you to do it now, or He wants you to start taking the necessary steps to get the ball in motion. Some things take a while to come to pass, so God will give you instruction in advance, but when God tells you to do something, you just do it. That's all there is to it.

The first time I drove through the tiny town of Pritchett on the eastern edge of Colorado, I was not impressed. The landscape was a flat, treeless plain as barren as any desert. The only shrubbery I could see was planted in people's yards, which didn't exactly provide lush green scenery considering only 140 people lived in the entire town. It looked like the end of the earth to me. I started joking with a friend who was in the car with me about how God was going to send him to this small village on the edge of nowhere.

"Thus saith the Lord," I told him. "You're being called to Pritchett, Colorado." We had a good time laughing about that. If it wasn't the edge of the world, you could see it from there—it was that close.

I stopped in Pritchett to preach at a church of ten people. We saw a man raised from the dead, and church attendance jumped up to around 100 people. They wanted me to stay and continue teaching them the full Gospel.

"You can't just come in here, challenge everything we thought we knew about God, and then leave town," they said.

I just laughed and said, "No way, I am *not* moving to Pritchett!"

No part of me wanted to live in Pritchett, but as we were driving out of town, I began to sense in my heart that God was telling me to stay there and teach the people the Word. By the time we got back to our house in Childress, Texas, I knew I was supposed to move. From a purely logical standpoint, there was no reason for me to go. The church only had ten members, they had no money, the church building was too small, and the town had nothing going for it. I could have given you a thousand reasons why it didn't seem like a good idea.

How could I fulfill my big vision in such a small place? Pritchett wasn't on the way to anywhere. It wasn't a stepping-stone to something better. It was a dead end. The only way to leave Pritchett was feet first, in a coffin. That's exactly the way I felt.

On the other hand, I was prospering in Childress, Texas. For the first time since I started in ministry, it looked like I might succeed. We had food and money on a regular basis, and things were going well for us. Our church had 50 or 60 people in regular attendance, I had a broadcast on the local radio station, and our church was making a difference. Everything was going great.

But once I knew that God wanted me to move to Pritchett, Colorado, the debate was over. Jesus is Lord of my life, and my attitude was that if God wanted me to do something, then I was going to do it—and enjoy doing it. Once I was convinced of God's will for me to move to Pritchett, I began to praise Him for leading and guiding me. Within days my entire attitude had changed, and I was excited about going. There were some hardships associated with living in such a remote area, but I loved living in Pritchett as much as any place I've ever lived. It was wonderful.

I made Jesus Lord of my life on March 23, 1968, and I haven't tried to direct my own life since. God is Lord, I'm not, and He knows what's best for me. I have feelings and opinions like everybody else, but the discussion ends once I'm sure God is telling me to do something. I trust God's judgment more than I trust my own, and I just do what He leads me to do. I couldn't even tell you how many decisions I've made in my life based purely on the fact that I was sure God was leading me.

It would really simplify your life to run up a white flag and surrender to Jesus as Lord. One of my favorite passages of Scripture is from Jeremiah. Jeremiah was wondering out loud how a people whom God rescued from Egypt and preserved through many miracles could forget the Lord who delivered them and turn to vain idols. In the middle of his grieving, Jeremiah answered his own question by saying,

> *O LORD, I know that the way of man is not in himself: it is not in man that walketh to direct his steps.*

Jeremiah 10:23

The Jews had fallen from a position of favor because they started doing things their own way. Jeremiah recognized that God didn't create us to rule our own lives. He gave us the free will to make our own choices, but God never intended for us to direct our own steps. We have the freedom to decide for ourselves, because God doesn't force His will upon us, but the correct choice is to recognize our complete dependency on God. We aren't smart enough to run our own lives. God said,

> *I call heaven and earth to record this day against you, that I have set before you life and death, blessing and cursing: therefore choose life, that both thou and thy seed may live.*

Deuteronomy 30:19

God gives us a choice, but He also tells us which option is best: He says, "Choose life!" Trust in the Lord with all your heart, and don't try to figure things out on your own. Seek His will in everything you do, and He'll show you the path to take—that's the smart choice (Proverbs 3:5-6). That's how we're supposed to live; we're meant to make Jesus our Lord and follow His guidance.

The world would be a different place if Adam and Eve had followed this philosophy. It was very clear that the serpent was enticing them to do something contrary to what God had told them, but they didn't follow God's guidance. They knew God as their Creator and recognized His provision for them, but they didn't submit to God as Lord of their lives. They knew He was kind to them, that He met with them and talked with them, but they didn't bow to Him and determine that they wouldn't lean unto their own understanding. They failed to surrender to God's sovereignty, and Satan went right through that open door to lead them into sin.

A solid Christian philosophy requires believing in the Word of God as your supreme authority and making Jesus Lord of your life. Not merely in the sense of recognizing His authority and attributes, but by submission to His leadership.

A rich man once kneeled down before Jesus and said, "Good Master, what must I do to inherit eternal life?"

"Why do you call Me good?" Jesus replied, "None is good except God alone." In other words, Jesus was saying, "Either call Me God and make Me Lord, or quit calling Me good!"

The rich man responded by calling Jesus "Master" again. He wasn't willing to go all the way and make Jesus his Lord and Savior. He wanted the salvation Jesus provides, but he didn't want to completely commit himself to following Jesus as Lord. Jesus knew the man wasn't totally sincere, but He still loved him. Jesus said, "Go, sell everything you have, and give the proceeds to the poor; it will give you treasure in heaven. Then come, take up your cross, and follow Me." The rich man couldn't do it, and he walked away grieved (Mark 10:17-22).

Jesus presented salvation as making Him Lord and Master over our lives—not just acknowledging His greatness. Scripture says that in order to be saved, you have to confess with your mouth that Jesus is Lord, and believe in your heart that God raised Him from the dead (Romans 10:9-10). I believe that salvation should be presented as turning your life over to Jesus—lock, stock, and barrel—but that's not how salvation is usually presented. The message many people are hearing is that they should be saved just so they can go to heaven when they die. Obviously, that is an important part of salvation, but it isn't the whole message. As a result, a lot of born-again believers will go to heaven when they die, but they haven't submitted to Jesus as Director and Leader of their everyday lives.

In my own case, I was born again when I was eight years old, but I didn't submit to Jesus as Lord until I was 18. During that ten-year interval, I believe I was born again. I loved God, and I had a relationship with Him to the degree that I would have gone to heaven if I had died, but I wasn't allowing Jesus to direct my life. I didn't submit to Jesus as Lord until March 23, 1968. I haven't lived perfectly since that time—obviously—but whenever I know God is telling me to do something, I do it. I yield to Jesus as my Lord, and my submission has led to a blessed life. Everything I set my hand unto prospers. God is a good God, and He leads me along good paths.

I believe this philosophy is absolutely essential. You need to adopt this way of thinking: You are going to do whatever God tells you to do, regardless of any other factors. Whether it is through the Word of God, or by special instruction from the Holy Spirit, decide ahead of time that you are going to follow God's leading; no discussion, no debate.

Over the years I have discovered that God will tell me to do things, but if I don't do them right away, He doesn't argue with me. He just tells me what He wants me to do, and then I have the choice of whether or not to follow Him. To the best of my ability, I do what God tells me to do, but if I miss His leadership, He won't debate the issue with me. So if you're waiting for God to convince you to do the thing you already know He wants you to do, you'll be waiting a long time because it isn't going to happen. God doesn't get into debates with us over His will for our lives. He will lead, and He will direct, but He isn't going to argue with you about what you already know.

Doing whatever we want and asking God to bless it as an afterthought, is not the same thing as following God. God tells us to do things for our own good. Really, being a Christian is simple. All you have to do is make Jesus Lord of your life, follow the leading of the Holy Spirit, and do what God's Word tells you to do. You'll solve a lot of problems in your life by following those few simple steps.

In order to remain sensitive to God's leading, we have to guard our hearts against the negative philosophies that are being promoted in the world. Every time you watch a television program, read a book, listen to the radio, browse the Internet, or watch a movie, you encounter ideas that are contrary to God's philosophy. Satan uses words to attack us through the way we think, and the modern media is the ideal way to push the world's philosophy. Every time you encounter those lies, you need to reject them. Isaiah says,

> *No weapon that is formed against thee shall prosper; and every tongue that shall rise against thee in judgment thou shalt condemn. This is the heritage of the servants of the Lord, and their righteousness is of me, saith the Lord.*
>
> *Isaiah 54:17*

The promise here is that attacks against us won't succeed. Notice that Isaiah then mentions the words spoken against us. The number one weapon Satan uses against us is deceitful words; he steals from people through vain philosophies and lies. This scripture says we are to "condemn" the lies that rise against us. The word "condemn" is defined by the American Heritage Dictionary as, "To express disapproval of, denounce; to convict; to sentence to a punishment; to declare unfit for use."

We have to take the authority God has given us and condemn those negative words, philosophies, and thoughts. Anything that is contrary to God's Word must be rejected.

This is more important than most of us realize. Most people go through the day hardly paying attention to all of the garbage, unbelief, doubt, and complaining that comes at us through the media and that wanders through our minds. All of those words and thoughts will corrupt you. Scripture says,

> *Be not deceived: evil communications corrupt good manners.*
>
> *1 Corinthians 15:33*

The truth of this scripture is demonstrated in the life of Lot and the infamous city of Sodom. Lot was a godly man, and the evil of the society he lived in was a continual grief to him, but his association with the city of Sodom cost him dearly. He never participated in their sins, but he ended up losing his wife and daughters in the judgment that came against Sodom (2 Peter 2:7-8). Lot is an example of the danger of trying to blend in and of the mistake in thinking that the evil in society around you won't affect you. You have to condemn the negative things around you.

Christians don't just wake up one morning and discover that they have a worldly philosophy; it happens slowly over time. We can see the process reflected in Satan's temptation of Eve. Satan didn't immediately call God a liar; he started out by questioning whether God had really told Eve not to eat of every tree in the Garden (Genesis 3:1). From there, he led Eve down a path of deceit until she was looking at things from his perspective, and finally disobeyed God's command. It's like the story of putting a frog into a boiling pot of water: the frog will jump out of the hot water immediately, but if you put that same frog in lukewarm water and turn the heat up very slowly, you can boil it alive and it will never try to escape because it won't notice the gradual temperature change. This is how the devil works. He doesn't come at us all at once; instead he drops little doubts here and there, and attacks the integrity of God's Word piece by piece.

I heard a story one time about a father who was trying to protect his kids from the influence of the world by monitoring the movies and television they watched. One day his daughter asked to go see a movie with her friends.

"What's it rated?" he asked.

"R," she mumbled in response.

"Well then, you can't go see it."

"But Dad," she argued, "Everyone says it's a great movie. All the other kids at church have seen it."

"What's in the movie that makes it rated R?" he asked.

"I'm not sure," she said. "I've heard there is a little nudity and some swearing, but not much. And it's supposed to be a great movie."

"I'm sorry honey, but I can't let you go see it," the father said.

The daughter was angry, but her dad wouldn't budge, so she had her friends come over to the house that night instead. While she was hanging out with her friends and playing games, her father made everyone brownies. After everything was set, they all lined up to get dessert.

"Now before you eat," he said over the excitement, "I just want to let you know that I put a little bit of dog poop in the recipe this time. It's not much. You probably won't taste it, and it won't make you sick or anything—but it is in there. Don't worry about it though—for the most part, these are really tasty brownies." I seriously doubt those kids ate any brownies. No matter how little dog poop ends up in your dessert, it's still spoiled. Why should we be any more tolerant of ungodliness in our entertainment?

The world we live in is fallen and corrupt, but many of us have accepted the condition of the world, and have grown tolerant of the ungodliness that surrounds us. We watch the same movies and television programs, read the same books, and listen to the same music—even though we know they aren't exactly right. We know they don't meet God's standard, but it's just a little bit of ungodliness; it's just a little nudity or profanity. Repeated exposure to that stuff leads to an increased tolerance for worldly viewpoints until, eventually, you are indulging attitudes and beliefs that are totally contrary to a godly perspective.

Our great-grandparents would be shocked to see the things that are on television and in magazines today. My wife and I have had a subscription to Reader's Digest magazine for years, and traditionally it has been a very wholesome family-oriented publication. Recently, they have begun including racy advertisements like those that feature the backs of nude women. It isn't nudity exactly, but it shows how the magazine is taking a step in the direction of more relaxed moral standards. Today, many popular magazines feature ads that would have been considered pornography a few generations ago.

I don't watch a lot of television, but I have an hour drive from my house into the office and I listen to the news on the radio. I don't listen to it for long though, because most of it is false proph-esy. They take a small event and blow it up by focusing on all of the negative things that *could* happen—usually with an emphasis on how it *will* happen, and maybe it will happen *to you*. You can ask anybody who rides in the car with me, I condemn the negative words that I hear over the radio.

When the news broadcast comes on and says, "It's flu season out there…Have you had your flu shot?" I say, "Oh, no it isn't. In the name of Jesus, it's not flu season for me." To the commer-cial that asks, "Are you having such-and-such medical problem? We can help…," I say, "No, thank you Jesus, I'm not having that problem."

I talk back to the radio and defend my belief system. I believe that when you hear a philosophy that is contrary to God's Word, you have to stand against it—that's what Eve should have done. When Satan said, "Did God really say…," Eve should have said, "Yes, God did say, and He is not a liar—so go away."

This might all sound a little weird, but it's just a component of guarding your heart. Scripture says we should guard our hearts above everything else in life, because our hearts determine the course of our lives (Proverbs 4:23). Satan tries to come against us through the way we think, so when I hear a lie, I condemn it. Condemn means to express disapproval of or denounce, and that's what I do—I speak the truth from God's Word to counter the lie. It's a part of guarding my heart.

When the media says sickness is rampant, I confess that by Jesus' stripes I'm healed (Isaiah 53:5; 1 Peter 2:24). When the newspaper says the economy is in the toilet, I flush that thought and confess that God supplies all my needs according to His riches in glory (Philippians 4:19). When I fall short and thoughts of condemnation rise up, I confess that there is no longer condemnation for those who are in Christ Jesus and walk after the spirit (Romans 8:1). Wherever and whenever the enemy attacks God's Word with a lie, I counter the lie by speaking the truth (John 17:17).

This is just a practical application of two philosophies I have been discussing. First, we have to believe that the Word of God is inspired and without error. Second, Jesus is Lord, and we shouldn't question His instructions. Those two philosophies will prevent Satan from having any access to us. Whenever you hear something that is contrary to God's Word, just reject it.

The philosophy of making Jesus Lord means that when God tells you to do something, you just do it. Unfortunately, many Christians debate with God whether or not they are going to do what He asks. For instance, Scripture says you're supposed to give, and the tithe (or 10% or your income) is just a starting place. Ten percent was the requirement under the Old Covenant. Nothing is required under the New Covenant of grace, but we should *desire* to give even more. God has promised that if we seek His Kingdom first, He will freely give us the food, clothing, and shelter we need (Matthew 6:33). Most Christians give a little from the abundance of their wealth, but they don't give joyfully. Scripture says,

How Do I Follow God?

Every man according as he purposeth in his heart, so let him give; not grudgingly, or of necessity: for God loveth a cheerful giver. And God is able to make all grace abound toward you; that ye, always having all sufficiency in all things, may abound to every good work.

2 Corinthians 9:7-8

A lot of people don't trust God to supply their needs, so they cling to money and material possessions as their safety net. They don't give joyfully because they are afraid God won't come through on His promise to give back. We have to trust God that His Word is a sure promise. No marriage or friendship can thrive unless the partners trust one another, and a relationship with God is no different in that respect. Following Jesus means trusting Him to do what He says He will do.

But many people who say "Jesus is Lord" prove by their actions that they don't really trust Him. The Bible tells us to love our enemies, to bless those who curse us, to do good to those who hate us, and to pray for those who persecute us and despitefully use us (Matthew 5:44). We know we're supposed to turn the other cheek, and we teach that principle to our children, but how many of us instantly slide into gossip and anger when someone comes against us? When we do that, we aren't submitting to Jesus as Lord of our lives. Our actions prove who is really sitting on the throne.

I'm not saying you can be perfect after you submit to Jesus as Lord, or that any failure in your life means you haven't submitted to Jesus. It isn't possible for us to live perfectly. We're still going to make mistakes. Even though our spirits are perfect, our bodies and souls won't be perfected until the Lord comes back and gives us glorified bodies and new souls. But our desire should be to follow Jesus' commands perfectly. Whenever we recognize that we are doing something contrary to the Word, we need to humble ourselves and turn back to God.

I certainly haven't lived perfectly. I've gossiped about people and said things in anger after someone has done something to hurt me. I've sinned plenty, but the moment I realize I am behaving contrary to God's instructions, I humble myself and turn away from whatever I was doing. My desire is that Jesus reigns as Lord of my life, and I follow His commands.

We are in a battle. We win eternal life when we are born again, but in this world we still have to fight the lies that come against us (Ephesians 6:12-13). We win those battles by making the determination that Jesus will reign as Lord in our lives, and by submitting to His leadership. When God leads us to do something, then we need to do it. The debate should end once God's will is clear in any area of our lives. No matter what the circumstances look like, we should follow God. The only way the enemy can win is for us to consider and submit to his lies instead of follow God's leading. God didn't create us to run our own lives. He gave us the freedom to make our own choices in life, but He also told us that the right option is to choose life. The correct choice is to use our free will to make Jesus Lord, and to follow His leading.

The great heroes of the Bible were people who followed God's way of thinking, even when it meant putting their life on the line. Shadrach, Meshach, and Abednego come immediately to mind; they were three young men who had been taken to Babylon during the captivity. After Daniel correctly interpreted one of King Nebuchadnezzar's dreams, he and Shadrach, Meshach, and Abednego were elevated to positions of leadership within the king's government. After some time, the king made an idol of gold and instructed everyone to bow down and worship it. When Shadrach, Meshach, and Abednego refused, they were brought before the king to be punished. The king told them that if they bowed down and worshipped the image he would let them live, but if they refused, he would throw them into a burning furnace. Then he challenged them by saying, "Who is the God who will deliver you from my hands then?"

They replied, "O Nebuchadnezzar, we are not careful to answer thee in this matter. If it be so, our God whom we serve is able to deliver us from the burning fiery furnace, and he will deliver us out of thine hand, O king. But if not, be it known unto thee, O king, that we will not serve thy gods, nor worship the golden image which thou hast set up" (Daniel 3:16-18).

Shadrach, Meshach, and Abednego knew God was capable of saving them, but they didn't have a specific promise that He *would*. Still, they were not afraid of the king's threats, so they told him that they were going to follow God, and they didn't care what he said or did about it. It didn't matter to them that the king was planning to roast them alive. They demonstrated that their commitment to God went beyond all other considerations, even the desire to live.

Most of us have not made such a strong commitment to God. Many will serve God and talk about the Gospel as long as they aren't persecuted, but as soon as someone starts making fun of them, they shrink back. When friends start deserting them and family members call them fanatics, they back off preaching the Gospel. As long as your philosophy allows for you to back down from your commitment to God, then the devil is going to have an inroad into your life. The enemy will use your concern over other people's opinions to manipulate you into conforming to his worldview. All he will have to do to stop you from following God's will for your life is bring people along to make fun of you. That's why the Bible says,

> *The fear of man bringeth a snare: but whoso putteth his trust in the LORD shall be safe.*

> Proverbs 29:25

Shadrach, Meshach, and Abednego maintained a philosophy that God is absolute Lord. He was the only one they would serve, and they would bow to no one else. Of course, their reply infuriated King Nebuchadnezzar. He was so angry that he ordered the furnace to be heated seven times hotter than usual. The king ordered the strongest men in his army to tie up Shadrach, Meshach, and Abednego and throw them into the fire—and the fire was so hot that the king's men were killed by the flames as they tossed the three Hebrews into the furnace.

The king gazed into the flames, watching to see the three Israelites consumed by the fire, but soon stood up in amazement and said, "Didn't we cast three men into the fire?" His advisors said, "Certainly we did, sir." And the king said,

> *Lo, I see four men loose, walking in the midst of the fire, and they have no hurt; and the form of the fourth is like the Son of God.*

> *Daniel 3:25*

In astonishment, the king went near to the fiery furnace, calling the names of Shadrach, Meshach, and Abednego, and ordering them to come out of the fire. They walked out from the middle of the flames and Scripture says, "…the princes, governors, and captains, and the king's counselors, being gathered together, saw these men, upon whose bodies the fire had no power, nor was an hair of their head singed, neither were their coats changed, nor the smell of fire had passed on them" (Daniel 3:27). The flames that consumed the king's strongest men had zero effect upon the three Hebrews who were totally committed to God.

Shadrach, Meshach, and Abednego refused to compromise, and God preserved them. Daniel was preserved in the same way when he was thrown into a den of lions after refusing to follow a law that forbade praying to God (Daniel 6). These biblical stories illustrate that commitment to God can't be a negotiable issue. Whatever you have to compromise to keep or obtain, you will eventually lose. Compromise is the language of the devil. You need to make the decision that Jesus is Lord, and you are going to remain absolutely committed to Him no matter what anyone else says or does—it's a necessary step in becoming grounded in a Christian worldview.

God should be our number one priority every day, but with many of us, He gets pushed to the end of our agenda. We should be seeking God about how to plan our days instead of planning our days and then seeing if we can squeeze in time for relationship with God. We should spend some time asking God, "What do *You* want me to do today?" We should present our calendar to God and say, "Here's my schedule God, what would *You* like me to do?" This is how God intended for us to live when He created us. We should be allowing the Lord to direct our steps, not trying to figure out life with our limited understanding.

A common misconception in the church today is that only really devout Christians need to make a total commitment to God. You might think what I'm suggesting is just for the minority of "super-saints" whom God has given a special grace to excel in the Lord's work, but that isn't true. There are no super-saints. All believers have received an abundance of grace to reign in this life as kings and queens (Romans 5:17). Making Jesus Lord of your life and believing that the Word of God is the absolute authority are simply basic steps in establishing a godly perspective. These are simple ideas that are foundational components of a Christian philosophy, and adopting this philosophy will radically change your life.

This may come as a surprise, but God's plans for your life are better than your plans for your life. You can trust Him. He desires good things for you (Jeremiah 29:11). The commands the Bible gives us about how to approach life are for our own good. It really simplifies life once you submit to Jesus as Lord and follow His commands regardless of what you think, feel, or see going on around you. Just make the decision that you are going to do what the Word says and follow the leadership of the Holy Spirit no matter what, and you will experience a drastic improvement in your quality of life.

Chapter Six

Can I Really Know God?

When Satan tempted Adam and Eve, he didn't come right out and call God a liar; he started by questioning, "Did God really say...." It wasn't until after he planted doubt in their minds that he accused God of lying to them. Satan told them that the real reason the Lord didn't want them to eat the fruit was because they would become like God (Genesis 3:5). The devil acted like God was being selfish; as if God didn't really love them, and didn't have their best interests in mind. It was a total slander against the true nature and character of God.

Why didn't Adam and Eve recognize that Satan was lying to them? I believe that although they communed with God in ways that most of us would long for, Adam and Eve didn't truly know God. I know that sounds like a radical statement—I struggled with it at first too. After all, Adam and Eve were perfect before sin entered the world. They walked with God in the cool of the evening and talked with Him. They weren't exposed to the ungodliness that has hardened our hearts toward God since sin entered the world. Everything was perfect, and nothing was blocking their relationship with God—but Adam and Eve didn't know the true

101

nature and character of God as well as we can today. They didn't know God loved them so much that He would become a man Himself, suffer humiliation, and lay down His life to save them. They knew God as Lord, but they didn't know Him as Savior.

The Word reveals to us the depths of God's love. It shows how God has pursued mankind throughout history; how He has loved us, and proven through His actions a love that Adam and Eve could not have imagined. True Christianity is the only religion on the face of the earth with the concept of God becoming a man and taking the punishment we deserved in order to redeem us and bring us back to a right relationship with Him.

Other religions may acknowledge a god-like entity, but they put the burden of salvation on the individual; on living a holy life, and meeting certain standards of righteousness. The standards vary, but one consistent theme among all man-made religions is that there are specific instructions you must follow to appease an angry god. True Christianity is all about *what God has already done for us*; it's not about what we do, or how we live. It's all about what God has done to give us *His* righteousness. The Gospel of John sums it up by saying,

> *For God so loved the world, that he gave his only begotten Son, that whosoever believeth in him should not perish, but have everlasting life.*
>
> John 3:16

God demonstrated His love for us when He sent Jesus to suffer and die for our sins, and then resurrected Him to give us His righteousness. It's a love that was impossible for Adam and Eve to understand. The sheer humility of God's plan of redemption is beyond human comprehension. No man could have conceived such a thing. Adam and Eve didn't know God's love to the extent that we can know and experience His love today. They had no idea that God would sacrifice His own Son so that they and their descendants could live forever. If they had known God that intimately, Satan would not have been able to deceive them into believing God was holding out on them, or trying to keep them from reaching their full potential.

A major part of having a Christian worldview is knowing God intimately, not from a distance. We can't just adapt other people's opinions about the nature and character of God. We need to have our own personal relationship with Him. The more we know the goodness of God, the less susceptible we will be to the lies of the devil. I fully believe that we succeed and experience victory in life to the degree that we have relationship with God. The good news is that we can know God better than Adam and Eve knew Him because we have a much greater revelation of the extent to which God will go for us. Therefore, we don't have to fall prey to the lies of the devil. Once you know God intimately, Satan won't be able to discredit Him or convince you that God can't move in your life. So a close, intimate, personal relationship with God is an essential component of a Christian philosophy.

The heroes of the Old Testament didn't understand God's love the way we can today. Prior to the resurrection and the gift of the Holy Spirit, not even Jesus' disciples had the revelation of God that is given to us in Scripture. At the crucifixion, the disciples were expecting Jesus to come down from the cross and establish His kingdom on earth. They didn't understand what was happening. When Jesus was arrested, the disciples ran away in fear and hid (Matthew 26:56; Mark 14:50). They knew Jesus was the Messiah, but they were expecting Him to establish a physical kingdom on earth—right then. As they stood and looked at Jesus hanging on the cross, they saw defeat. To them, it looked like all of the hope they had placed in Jesus to save mankind was wasted. It shocked them when Jesus rose from the dead because they didn't know or understand God's plan of salvation (Mark 16:11; Luke 24:11; John 20:9, 25).

In hindsight, through the record of Scripture, I now have a greater understanding of why Jesus sacrificed Himself on the cross than His disciples had prior to the coming of the Holy Spirit. Even after the establishment of the Church, Peter—one of the Lord's closest disciples—still didn't fully understand grace or the dynamics of what had happened on the cross. He was trying to merge the Christian faith back into Jewish law and the apostle Paul had to openly rebuke him for it (Galatians 2:11-14). Years later, Peter wrote in his second letter:

> ...our beloved brother Paul also according to the wisdom given unto him hath written unto you; As also in all his epistles, speaking in them of these things; in which are some things hard to be understood, which they that are unlearned and unstable wrest, as they do also the other scriptures, unto their own destruction.

2 Peter 3:15-16

Peter says right here that Paul's revelation of Jesus was superior to his own. Peter lived with Jesus for three and a half years, and Paul spent no time with Jesus while He was walking on earth, yet Paul had a greater revelation of who Jesus was and what He came to accomplish. The point is that Paul didn't get his revelation from other people, he received it through his spirit—the same way we receive revelation today. Paul has recorded for us the revelation God gave him in the letters he composed, which make up half of the New Testament. Through the Holy Spirit and the study of Scripture, we can know God's love for us to a degree that the disciples of Jesus did not understand while they were ministering with Him on earth. That's an amazing statement!

I have a greater revelation of the true nature of God than Abraham or Moses had—not because I'm better than they were, but because God's plan of redemption is complete, and I have a fuller picture of God than they did. If I could travel back in time and sit down with Moses to explain God's plan of redemption, he wouldn't understand it. He wouldn't understand that the system of animal sacrifice they practiced was only foreshadowing how God would send His Son to live in the flesh and become the Lamb who takes away the sins of the world. Moses did not anticipate that God would do away with the sacrificial system and tear down the veil that separated us from the holy of holies. He had no idea those things would happen.

Jesus said that John the Baptist was the greatest of those born of women, but "...he that is least in the kingdom of heaven is greater than he" (Matthew 11:11). Our born-again spirits make us greater than any of the Old Testament prophets. Greater than men like Moses, who spent 40 days and nights in the presence of God, and when he returned to the Israelites his face was radiating the glory of God; like Abraham, who believed God and became the father of faith; like Elijah, who called down fire from heaven and never died but was taken up to heaven in a chariot of fire; like Joshua, who led God's people into the Promised Land; and like David, who was a man after God's own heart. We have access to a greater revelation of God's true nature than any of those men had.

Scripture says the Old Covenant, written and engraved in stone, led to death—but it was also glorious. When Moses presented the Law to the people of Israel, they couldn't bear to look at him because of the brightness of God's glory that was reflected in his face. The old way was glorious, but what we have is much more glorious. Under the New Covenant, the Holy Spirit gives us life forever, which is infinitely better than the death that came through the Law (2 Corinthians 3:6-11).

The revelation we have of God's love should cause us to trust Him. We shouldn't be susceptible to the lies of the devil in the same way that Adam and Eve were. Satan was able to slander God's character because Adam and Eve didn't really know God, but we *do* know Him. God has proven His love for us. The apostle Paul wrote,

> *He that spared not his own Son, but delivered him up for us all, how shall he not with him also freely give us all things?*

> *Romans 8:32*

Once we truly understand the extent of God's love for us, demonstrated through the sacrifice of Jesus, we won't doubt His desire to freely give us all things. Jesus has completely redeemed us, and a full revelation of that truth will naturally lead you to believe how much God desires to bless you financially, heal you physically, and give you all that you need. The greater your revelation of God's love, the more successful you will be at resisting the attacks of the enemy.

From what I can see, most Christians do not have an intimate relationship with the Lord. They know God from a distance, through the things they have heard from their pastor or someone else, but they don't know God for themselves. Before I understood that God loves me because His nature is love, and not because I am lovely, I was always trying to do things to earn God's favor. When I was doing good, I felt close to God, but when I was falling short—which was most of the time—I didn't feel close to Him. All I could see was my own unworthiness. But once I got a revelation of how much God loves me, independent of my actions, everything that was holding me back from relationship with Him disappeared.

One of the greatest truths of Christianity is that your relationship with God is the key to everything. It's the key to having joy, peace, and abundance. It's the way to experiencing victory in life. Yet most believers aren't taking advantage of this amazing gift of relationship that is available to us.

After my encounter with God on March 23, 1968, I intuitively knew that God loved me, completely separate from what I deserved, and it lit a fire under me to pursue relationship with Him even further. But even though I knew God loved me, I didn't understand His love. I made a total commitment to God that day, but it took years for me to understand how a holy God could love me. I had spent my entire life trying to make myself righteous and acceptable to God, and I just couldn't get my mind around the fact that God's love and acceptance had nothing to do with my own efforts.

I was raised in a legalistic, works-oriented, religious system. My father died when I was twelve years old, and my church told me God killed him because it was His will for my father to die. I was taught that God put sickness, disease, poverty, and depression on us as punishments to make us better people. I was told that the more you suffer, the holier you become. All of those ideas are absolutely false, but I didn't know any better back then. After my encounter with God's love, I was totally committed to God, but I had a wrong understanding of what God might do to make my relationship with Him deepen. It can be dangerous to be a living sacrifice—being totally submitted to the will of God—when you don't know what God's will includes! This is another reason why it's important to renew your mind (Romans 12:1-2).

I won't go into all of the details, but a few years after I made myself a living sacrifice, a traveling preacher came to my church and prophesied over me that God was going to put me into a coma. He told me that I was going to get sick and enter a vegetative state for years. He droned on and on about how God was going to use sickness to break me, but I would emerge as strong as the apostle Paul after I came through it. I was ready to submit to what he said was God's will for me. Satan had me on the ropes. I was ready to accept whatever God wanted for me. But then the devil went too far. The so-called prophet told me that after I emerged from the coma, God was going to make me abstain from reading the Word for eight years.

I didn't know much, but I had a relationship with God and I knew He would never tell me not to read His Word. As soon as the preacher said that, I knew it was all a lie. I stood up, renounced everything he had spoken over me, and walked away. I believe that if I would have submitted to that false prophecy, I would have entered into a coma and died.

God doesn't use sickness to make people better; the devil uses sickness to steal, kill, and destroy (John 10:10). Scripture tells us to submit to God and resist the devil, and the devil will flee (James 4:7). But if we submit to the attacks of the enemy and fail to resist evil, then the devil won't flee. I was able to resist the lies that were being spoken over me because I knew God. I had experienced the Word of God coming alive, God had spoken to me through it, and I knew He wouldn't take that away from me.

As New Covenant believers, we are able to understand the depths of God's love better than anyone did prior to the resurrection of Christ Jesus. Adam and Eve fell for Satan's temptation because they didn't know God well enough to realize that Satan was lying to them. If they had known God better, they would have recognized that He would never withhold good from them. Knowing God helps keep us from being deceived and from having our faith in God undermined by misunderstandings or wrong teaching.

I've been married to my wife Jamie since 1972. A lot of people may know Jamie, but I know her intimately. If someone were to tell me a story about Jamie that is totally inconsistent with her personality, I would know it wasn't true because I know the kinds of things she would say and do. When you know someone well, it keeps you from being deceived by gossip or slander. But when you only know someone casually, you are more likely to believe the things you hear about them simply because you don't have any firsthand knowledge to judge by. The same is true of your relationship with God.

This analogy breaks down a little because people aren't perfect, and sometimes they do things that are inconsistent with their normal behavior, but with God there are no exceptions. God is the same yesterday, today, and forever (Hebrews 13:8). God says, "For I am the LORD, I change not" (Malachi 3:6). God is always the same. He doesn't make us righteous by grace one day, and then judge us by our performance the next. So when religion tries to claim that God doesn't want to heal every person, or that He puts sickness on people to teach them a lesson, we can know that those ideas are inconsistent with His nature. Jesus was the perfect representation of God (John 14:7, 9; Hebrews 1:3), and He went around doing good and healing *all* who were oppressed by the devil (Acts 10:38). We can know God's true nature because He reveals it to us in His Word.

People tend to think it would be great to have the same relationship with God that Old Testament kings and prophets had—like Adam and Eve, who walked with God in the cool of the evening; or Moses who went up on a mountain and spent 40 days in the presence of God. Those were awesome privileges to be sure, but the revelation of God's true nature that has been given to us in Scripture is better than the revelation they had. We can actually know God better than they did. We can even know God better than the apostles knew Him prior to Jesus' resurrection and the gift of the Holy Spirit.

It's important for us to base our philosophy on the revelation of Jesus Christ and His grace, and not upon the traditions or ideas of men. Probably the most damaging tradition that is circulating in the body of Christ is the idea that nothing can happen unless God wills it to happen. That is a wrong philosophy, and it causes a lot of unnecessary pain. It isn't God's will for some babies to be born with deformities. God doesn't desire war, rape, or violence. God isn't behind any of the evil that we see in this world. Scripture says that God cannot be tempted with evil, and He doesn't tempt us with evil either (James 1:13). If you think God is sovereignly determining everything that happens in life, then you're going to be susceptible to bitterness and doubt toward Him. You'll either be mad at Him for making such a terrible mess of the world, or you'll lack confidence in Him for being unwilling to prevent it.

But God doesn't control everything. He gave us control, but mankind is too busy cooperating with the devil to fix what's wrong. God is all-powerful, but He has chosen to work through us (Ephesians 3:20). God's will doesn't automatically come to pass. We have to cooperate with Him. If it was purely up to God, then everything on earth would be done the way it is in heaven (Matthew 6:10); there wouldn't be any sickness, crime, or sorrow. If God was controlling everything, our world wouldn't be in the mess it's in.

Anyone who is upset with God has a wrong philosophy. They have been influenced by religion or other false doctrines that have misrepresented the Lord. One of the largest television networks in the United States is run by a man whose sister died when they were both very young. The church he attended told him it was God's will for her to die, and he decided that he didn't want anything to do with a God who would kill his sister. A wrong philosophy turned him against God, and he used his media influence to attack the Judeo-Christian ethic in the United States. I understand why he feels the way he does, but he has a wrong impression of God.

The thief cometh not, but for to steal, and to kill, and to destroy: I am come that they might have life, and that they might have it more abundantly.

John 10:10

God doesn't kill anybody—it's the devil who takes lives. God comes to give us life in abundance. The Greek word used for life here is *zoe*, which means life that is active, vigorous, devoted to God, and blessed.[24] God is a good God! The Word also says,

> *Every good gift and every perfect gift is from above, and cometh down from the Father of lights, with whom is no variableness, neither shadow of turning.*

> *James 1:17*

The simplest Christian theology is that if something is good, then it comes from God; if it's bad, then it's from the devil. God is not the cause of the tragedy in our lives. He doesn't take away our loved ones or cause disabilities, and He doesn't control and predetermine everything in life.[25] One reason for this is that God doesn't want to interfere with our free will, because doing so would cut off our only path to salvation. Another reason is that He has given us authority over the attacks of the enemy, and He won't just step in and do things for us automatically. God uses people, so we need to cooperate with Him to allow His goodness and power to flow through us. Everything we need is already in our born-again spirits. When we cooperate with Him, His power flows from our spirits into our bodies and lives, bringing healing and victory.

---

[24] "Dictionary and Word Search for *zōē (Strong's 2222)*". *Blue Letter Bible*. 1996-2012. 7 January 2011. < http:// www.blueletterbible.org/lang/ lexicon/lexicon.cfm?Strongs=G2222&t=KJV >

[25] I have three lengthy teachings that will give you a much deeper understanding in this area: *Spirit, Soul, and Body*, *The Believer's Authority*, and *The True Nature of God*. Visit our website (www.awmi.net) and click on "Extras" to download free audio teachings, or order books from our online store.

God is your best friend—whether you recognize it or not. God is for you; He wants you to live a life full of joy and peace. Some people are afraid to seek God wholeheartedly because they think He might ask them to do something that would make them miserable, like move to the most remote corner of the globe and live under primitive conditions. They are afraid God will suck all of the joy out of their lives, but He won't. God would never do something to hurt you—just the opposite. Once you start delighting in God, you will find that the desires of your heart are God's desires also (Psalm 37:4-5). So if God leads you to go minister in a remote area, it's because you will fall in love with the people and love your work. God will always give you the grace to do what He calls you to do.

A life with God is an abundant, joyful life. The reason so many people are struggling today is that they don't really know the goodness of God. You can't base your relationship with God on what other people say, or their encounters with God. You have to know Him for yourself. God desires relationship with you, and relationship with God is the solution to any and every problem you might encounter.

We often emphasize the importance of seeking God, but the truth is that God is seeking us more than we have ever sought Him. All you have to do is slow down a little and make a half turn toward God, and He will come into your life in a big way. You can know God personally—by intimate relationship—beyond mere knowledge *about* Him. Once you know God for yourself, you won't fall for the devil's schemes. The enemy wants you to believe that life would be better if you had a bigger house, a nicer car, or a different spouse, but happiness is really found in relationship with the Lord.

God made us to desire relationship with Him. People who don't know God try to satisfy that desire with substitute pleasures; they lust after sexual relationships, take drugs, or drink alcohol. They look for happiness in collecting material possessions and in the praise of others. They continually search for a sense of fulfillment in achieving the next big goal. None of those things are ultimately satisfying. What every human being needs is relationship with God.

After God created Adam, He breathed His Spirit into him. We were designed to be filled with God's presence, but when Adam and Eve rebelled, they kicked God out of their lives. God wasn't only talking about physical death when He commanded Adam not to eat of the forbidden fruit. The Lord said, "...for in the day that thou eatest thereof thou shalt surely die" (Genesis 2:17), but Adam and Eve lived on earth for many years after their rebellion. The death they experienced was spiritual, which eventually resulted in physical death. Adam and Eve's rebellion caused a God-shaped vacuum to be formed inside of every person. Sex, drugs, money, success, fame, and the other pursuits society is caught up in, are just human attempts to fill the void caused by spiritual death.

We were made for relationship with God, and the only way to fill our spiritual void is to be born again and enter into relationship with Him. The reason I don't do drugs is that I'm not miserable. My born-again spirit allows me to enter into the presence of God and enjoy relationship with Him. In the presence of God is fullness of joy and pleasures forevermore (Psalm 16:11). You can get so full of God that you won't feel the need to be filled with anything else. The lust for other things will disappear. Once you have a real relationship with God, every day with Jesus can be sweeter than the day before.

Surface-level knowledge of God's love is not the same thing as plunging into the reality of His love. Real relationship with God involves going beyond a mere intellectual awareness of His love. Of all the things the apostle Paul could have prayed for the Ephesians, he prayed for them to know the love of God. He said:

> *For this cause I bow my knees unto the Father of our Lord Jesus Christ, Of whom the whole family in heaven and earth is named, That he would grant you, according to the riches of his glory, to be strengthened with might by his Spirit in the inner man; That Christ may dwell in your hearts by faith; that ye, being rooted and grounded in love, May be able to comprehend with all saints what [is] the breadth, and length, and depth, and height; And to know the love of Christ, which passeth knowledge, that ye might be filled with all the fulness of God.*
>
> *Ephesians 3:14-19*

This scripture shows that God's love has multiple dimensions; it isn't merely a fact that you memorize like trivia. You can be overwhelmed by the height, depth, length, and breadth of God's love so that it "passes knowledge," and becomes an experience of being filled with the grace and peace of God. It's one thing to say, "Oh yeah, I know God loves me." It's something else altogether to be filled with the fullness of God.

Do you know what it means to be filled with the fullness of God? God isn't depressed, discouraged, fearful, or anxious. He isn't poor or starving. The fullness of God is healing, prosperity, joy, peace, anointing, purpose, and total satisfaction. You get all of those things by *knowing* God experientially. In biblical language, "to know" is used to infer sexual intimacy. As in, "Adam knew Eve his wife; and she conceived, and bare Cain" (Genesis 4:1). The Greek word Paul used in his prayer for the Ephesians is the same word used to describe how Joseph abstained from intimate relations with Mary until after the birth of Jesus (Matthew 1:25). Paul prayed for an intimate personal knowledge of the love of Christ, one that passes mere knowledge, because that is how you get filled with the fullness of God.

Fear, loneliness, anger, frustration, poverty, sickness and anxiety simply reflect a lack of the fullness of God. The remedy for those things is a revelation of how much God loves you. You just need a deeper relationship with God; one that allows you to experience the love of Christ beyond mere knowledge *about* Him. Of the thousands of people I counsel and pray for, nearly all of them are struggling because they lack a deep personal relationship with God.

Christian Philosophy

Religion teaches people an approach to God that emphasizes personal effort, but no one can be perfect, and the frustration of failure leaves people feeling unlovable and separated from God. The Good News of Jesus Christ is that you don't have to *earn* relationship with God. Jesus earned it for us by dying on the cross and rising again. All of us were spiritually dead, unable to save ourselves, so Jesus came and died on our behalf to save us. He took our sin and gave us His righteousness. Salvation has nothing to do with what you deserve. God did this because He loves us and desires an intimate relationship with us.

Not every Christian has a deep personal relationship with God, but that isn't God's fault. It's because we've been lied to. We've been taught that we have to earn relationship with God by living a holy life, going to church every week, paying a tithe, and studying the Word. Most believers are stuck on a treadmill of trying to live up to the requirements of being a good Christian, falling short, and then getting back up to try harder. Their own hearts are condemning them and keeping them from entering into an intimate relationship. This is a wrong philosophy. Jesus paid for all of our sins—past, present, and future—and our shortcomings don't separate us from God. Scripture says,

> *For we through the Spirit wait for the hope of righteousness by faith. For in Jesus Christ neither circumcision availeth any thing, nor uncircumcision; but faith which worketh by love.*

> *Galatians 5:5-6*

Trying to earn God's love isn't going to get you anywhere. We're saved by faith, not by works. Once you rid yourself of the burden of thinking you have to be good enough and simply accept how much God loves you, your faith will go through the roof. Faith works by love, and faith is what releases the ability and the power of God. Knowing God's love will heal your body and bring peace to your mind. It will make your finances increase and your relationships flourish. Letting the love of God flow in you will bless you even beyond what you can imagine.

Maybe this sounds too good to be true. You might think there has to be more to it—some complicated step to perform—but it really is as simple as knowing God. Adam and Eve never experienced rejection or punishment from God prior to the Fall, but they never experienced the breadth, length, depth, and height of His love either. If they had known the fullness of God's love, then Satan would never have been able to tempt them.

Before any of us can be tempted to sin, Satan first has to make us dissatisfied with what we already have. Adam and Eve were living in a sinless and perfect world, yet a talking snake convinced them God was holding out on them. Think about that. The temperature was perfect, the food was perfect, they didn't have any financial problems, and Adam and Eve were both perfect. They weren't constantly being bombarded by media reports of killing and strife all over the world. They couldn't even complain about each other. Everything was perfect. Yet Satan was able to make Adam and Eve feel discontent in the middle of paradise. Imagine, then, how easy it is for him to make people in our fallen world feel unhappy.

We live in a world where there is plenty to be displeased about, but the truth is that through Jesus, we can experience the love of God to a greater degree than Adam and Eve ever did. We can be filled with all the fullness of God and feel completely satisfied. What a powerful truth! All of the things you desire from God come freely through a heart that knows how wide, how long, how high, and how deep God's love is. Relationship with God is the pathway to everything He desires to give you.

Even though Adam and Eve were living in sinless perfection, they had a deficiency in their relationship with God—they didn't know how much He loved them. Today, the shortages in our relationships with God are not because He hasn't communicated the depths of His love or His great desire to know us intimately. Our problem is that most of us aren't entering into the intimacy God is calling us to. Often, it's because we have a wrong philosophy and believe that we have to earn holiness in order to enter God's presence. The traditions and doctrines of men have made God's Word of no effect (Mark 7:13). Other times, we are simply too caught up in the things of this world to notice God calling us.

As a society, we are busy with many pursuits. So much stuff is being thrown at us every day that we don't have time to be still and know God (Psalm 46:10), and to know the greatness of His love for us. But it's within our power to change that. We can renew our minds and toss out the old religious philosophies that have damaged our relationship with God. We can set aside time to spend with God and get to know His love. The promise of God's Word is that if we draw close to God, He will draw close to us (James 4:8). Jesus said,

> *Ask, and it shall be given you; seek, and ye shall find; knock, and it shall be opened unto you: For every one that asketh receiveth; and he that seeketh findeth; and to him that knocketh it shall be opened.*

> *Matthew 7:7-8*

God wants a relationship with you more than you desire a relationship with Him, so it's not a matter of you trying hard enough and forcing God to acknowledge you. It's simply a matter of allowing God to love you. God desires intimacy with you, but you have to let it happen. You do that by seeking Him and yielding to His love. This understanding is essential to any Christian philosophy, and it will make a huge difference in the quality of life you experience.

Chapter Seven

Is God Angry with Me?

I remember watching an old game show on TV when I was a kid called *To Tell the Truth*. Three guests sat in front of a panel of four celebrity judges. All three of the guests claimed the same identity, but only one of them was the real person—the other two people were imposters trying to confuse the judges. For instance, all three of them would claim to be Joe Smith, a heavy weight boxer. One of the guests really would be Joe Smith, but the other two were just acting. After the judges asked a lot of questions, they would make guesses about which one of the guests they thought was telling the truth. When the judges were done guessing, the announcer would say, "Would the real 'Joe Smith' please stand up!" They would always have one person start to stand up and then another, and finally, the real Joe Smith would stand.

I think God is being represented in so many contrasting ways by so many different groups in society, that many people are frustrated and confused. They want to say, "Would the real God please stand up!" They read Old Testament scriptures that talk about God smiting people with leprosy, and then they hear someone like me say God is love and He would never use evil against us, and they wonder, "Which one is the real God?" They wonder if God is schizophrenic or something, but God has never changed. He has always been the same loving God we see manifested in the life and ministry of Jesus.

God is on our side, yet a lot of people think of Him as an old man with a long grey beard, leaning over a banister in heaven with a lightning bolt in His hand, ready to sock it to us the minute we step out of line. They imagine a harsh and angry God who is eager to judge us for the wrong we've done. Religion is even teaching that suffering and disease are a blessing in disguise—they say God uses evil to teach us a lesson (Isaiah 5:20). None of those statements are true, but many people are confused about what the truth really is.

To begin with, we have to understand the difference between the way God dealt with people under the Old Covenant, and the way He deals with us as born-again believers under the New Covenant. God revealed a mercy and grace through Jesus that you don't see in the Old Testament scriptures—but God hasn't changed, He has just changed the way He relates to mankind because of the transformation in *us*.

The Gospel of John tells the story of a woman who was caught in adultery by the Pharisees and brought to Jesus for judgment. It says,

> *Jesus went unto the mount of Olives. And early in the morning*
> *he came again into the temple, and all the people came unto*
> *him; and he sat down, and taught them. And the scribes and*

Pharisees brought unto him a woman taken in adultery; and when they had set her in the midst, they say unto him, Master, this woman was taken in adultery, in the very act. Now Moses in the law commanded us, that such should be stoned: but what sayest thou?

John 8:1-5

On the surface, the Pharisees appear to have been seeking justice by bringing the adulteress before Jesus, but they were really just trying to entrap Him. It's interesting that the woman was caught in the act of adultery, yet the Pharisees didn't apprehend the man she was with. Although we don't know for sure, I can think of two possible reasons for this. First, the man might have been someone the Pharisees enlisted to help capture the woman in the middle of the act—specifically for the purpose of setting this trap for Jesus. So they let the man escape because he was part of the deal. Second, if it really was a randomly discovered act of adultery, maybe they only brought the woman because we tend to be easier on women when it comes to sentencing people to death. The Old Testament Law said that a person caught in adultery should be stoned to death (Leviticus 20:10; Deuteronomy 22:22), and they might have thought bringing just the woman suited their purpose of entrapment better—figuring it would be harder for Jesus to condemn a woman than a man.

Jesus had been preaching and teaching the mercy of God, and He wanted to set people free from the bondage of religious tradition. Jesus ate meals with sinners (Matthew 9:11; Mark 2:16;

Luke 15:2), and associated with outcasts. One of His disciples was a hated tax collector (Matthew 10:3), and a formerly demon-possessed woman cooked for Him (Luke 8:2). His life and teaching were in complete contrast to the harsh, judgmental God that the religious leaders of the day were portraying.

By bringing this woman to Jesus for judgment, the Pharisees were trying to make Him choose between obeying the Law and demonstrating the mercy He had been preaching. Either way, they thought Jesus was trapped. If He demonstrated mercy and let the woman go, then He himself would be subject to stoning for failing to enforce the Law of Moses. Yet if Jesus followed the Law and condemned the woman to death, then He would be going against the message of mercy He had been teaching, and the people would think He was a hypocrite. The Pharisees thought it was a win-win situation.

Of course, the Pharisees' trap wasn't as good as they thought. Jesus immediately recognized what they were up to, so when the Pharisees threw the woman down before Jesus and demanded His judgment, Jesus simply bent down and wrote in the dirt with His finger. When the Pharisees continued to press Him for an answer, Jesus stood up and said, "He that is without sin among you, let him first cast a stone at her" (John 8:7). Then Jesus bent over again and continued writing on the ground. We don't know what He was writing, but whatever it was, it appears to have convicted the accusers of their own sins. One by one, they walked away until only the woman was left standing before Jesus. When Jesus looked up and saw only the woman, He said,

Is God Angry with Me?

Woman, where are those thine accusers? hath no man condemned thee? She said, No man, Lord. And Jesus said unto her, Neither do I condemn thee: go, and sin no more.

John 8:10-11

Jesus didn't tell the woman that it was okay to commit adultery. He didn't lower the standard of righteousness. Some people today are trying to reconcile God's love and holiness by saying everything is okay—drunkenness, adultery, homosexuality, drugs, and other harmful lifestyle choices—but that isn't how Jesus responded. He didn't deny the woman's act was wrong or imply that it would be okay for her to continue committing adultery. No, He said, "go and sin no more." Jesus admitted that she had sinned, but He didn't condemn her—He showed mercy.

Adultery was punishable by death under the Old Covenant, but Jesus didn't enforce the punishment. If someone was caught in adultery under the Law of Moses, they were stoned to death; it wasn't negotiable. As a matter of fact, the very first person who was punished for breaking the Old Testament Law was a man who gathered sticks on the Sabbath (Numbers 15:32-36). After he was caught gathering sticks, the Israelites turned him over to Moses and Aaron because no one knew what the punishment should be. The Lord told Moses that the man should be brought outside the camp and stoned to death. He was killed for gathering sticks to make a fire!

Some people hear these stories and they wonder, "Why the change?" In a nutshell, God held people accountable for sin under the Old Covenant, so He punished them for it. But under the New Covenant, our sins have all been paid for by Jesus, and God isn't holding sin against us anymore. God has changed the way He deals with us because the price for sin has been paid—and that single change makes everything brand new. After putting our faith in Jesus, we become new creatures (2 Corinthians 5:17), and God can deal with us differently than He could deal with people under the Old Covenant (Hebrews 8:12-13).

Jesus changed everything, and nothing has been the same since. A helpful illustration is to consider how we change the way we relate to our own children as they mature. Young children often have to be physically restrained from doing wrong. I know many people today reject spanking children as being harmful, but leaving children to themselves is what's harmful. The scripture says,

The rod and reproof give wisdom: but a child left to himself bringeth his mother to shame.

Proverbs 29:15

So, it's a godly thing to use corporal punishment to train young children. A two year old doesn't understand that the devil is inspiring our selfish actions. If you try and tell them that it's the devil who leads them to take their sibling's toy, they will just look at you with a blank stare. They don't get it.

But when the devil gives them those selfish thoughts of taking their sibling's toy, you can tell them, "If you do that again, I'm going to give you a spanking." They may not know about resisting the devil (James 4:7), but I guarantee you when that thought comes again, they will resist it because they don't want the punishment. Sometimes kids need to be spanked—not to hurt them, but to deter them from doing what is wrong.

Even so, spanking is not a long-term solution. You only use physical restraint for a short period of time until children grow up and you can teach them by instruction. We don't spank our 20-, 30-, or 40-year-old children! Likewise, the Old Testament revealed God's wrath against sin, and He put punishments in place to deter the Israelites from sinning until His plan of redemption could unfold. When the time was right, Jesus came and paid for our sin. Until Jesus made a new way for us, the Israelites were kept under the Law, waiting for saving faith in Christ to appear (Galatians 3:23). The apostle Paul said it this way:

> *Wherefore the law was our schoolmaster to bring us unto Christ, that we might be justified by faith. But after that faith is come, we are no longer under a schoolmaster.*
>
> *Galatians 3:24-25*

The Law was just a training tool God used to guide His children until we could be saved by faith. You could say that the human race was in its infancy until Jesus came and revealed the true nature of God. Before Jesus came, God dealt with sin harshly in order to keep the Israelites out of trouble. But now, God no longer deals with His children in the same way. We aren't under the Law the Israelites were under (Romans 6:14). We have a different covenant, a New Covenant of salvation by grace, through faith in Jesus (Ephesians 2:8). We are a different kind of people from the Old Covenant believers—new creatures entirely—and God deals with us differently.

It's true that God inflicted people with leprosy and destroyed entire cities under the Old Covenant, but those actions have to be understood within the context of how God was able to deal with humanity. Jesus changed all that. He made it possible for us to be spiritually reborn. In much the same way that you can't reason with an infant, God couldn't reason with humanity prior to Jesus. In the Old Testament, God released His wrath on people, but in the New Testament, Jesus changed how God relates to us.

Scripture says Jesus is the exact representation of God the Father (Hebrews 1:3). The Old Testament prophets revealed some truths about God, but Jesus gave us a complete view of the Father. The writer of Hebrews said "How shall we escape, if we neglect so great salvation; which at the first began to be spoken by the Lord, and was confirmed unto us by them that heard him" (Hebrews 2:3). Jesus revealed God in a way that superseded all previous revelation. In Jesus, we see a kind and compassionate God who gave Himself over to a cruel death, in order to give us the hope of new life.

Jesus' disciples tried to re-enact a story from the Old Testament once, and His response to them dramatically illustrates the difference between the Old and the New Covenants. The story revolves around the ungodly king Ahaziah—the son of Ahab and Jezebel. Ahaziah fell seriously ill, but instead of seeking the Lord for healing, he sent messengers to inquire about his recovery from

the false god Baalzebub, the god of the neighboring people of
Ekron. God told the prophet Elijah what king Ahaziah was doing
and sent him to intercept the messengers. Elijah said to them, "Is
it not because there is not a God in Israel, that ye go to enquire of
Baalzebub the god of Ekron? Now therefore thus saith the LORD,
Thou shalt not come down from that bed on which thou art gone
up, but shalt surely die" (2 Kings 1:3-4).

When the messengers heard this, they returned to Ahaziah
and reported what Elijah had said. Although Elijah didn't identify
himself to the messengers, he had a long history with Ahaziah's
family, and the king knew right away who it was that had spoken
to them. After hearing Elijah's warning, the king sent out a captain
with fifty soldiers to capture him. The captain found Elijah on top
of a hill and commanded him to come down. Elijah replied, "If
I be a man of God, then let fire come down from heaven, and
consume thee and thy fifty" (2 Kings 1:10). After saying this, fire
came down from heaven and consumed the captain and his fifty
soldiers.

Not deterred, the king sent out another captain with fifty soldiers. Elijah called down fire from heaven again, and the second
captain and his men were also killed. So the king sent out a third
captain with fifty soldiers, but this time the captain fell down on
his knees before Elijah and begged for his life. At that, the angel
of the Lord spoke to Elijah, told him not to be afraid, and to go
with the soldiers to see king Ahaziah. Elijah went with the men,
delivered a message to the king, and that was the end of the matter.

This story comes up again in the New Testament while Jesus and His disciples were passing through Samaria. The Jews looked down upon the Samaritans because they had stayed behind in the land of Israel and intermarried with Gentiles during the time the Jews were taken into captivity. As a result of the intermarrying, the Samaritans adopted pagan beliefs and mixed them with their Jewish religious tradition. Because of the Samaritan's mixed religion, the Jews forbade them from worshipping in Jerusalem—even though they were worshipping the God of Israel. The mutual hatred between the Jews and the Samaritans was both religious and racial, and we need to keep the extreme prejudice between them in mind as we read the New Testament story.

> *And it came to pass, when the time was come that he should be received up, he stedfastly set his face to go to Jerusalem, And sent messengers before his face: and they went, and entered into a village of the Samaritans, to make ready for him. And they did not receive him, because his face was as though he would go to Jerusalem.*
>
> *Luke 9:51-53*

We know Jesus had already taught in Samaria because the Gospel of John tells the story of Jesus ministering to the woman at the well (John 4). After Jesus ministered to the woman, she went and got the entire village to go hear Him, and they all accepted Him as the Messiah. On this occasion, Jesus was on His way to Jerusalem, but instead of going around Samaria the way the strict Jews did, He went right through Samaria. Before arriving,

Jesus sent some men ahead to find Him lodging, but once the Samaritans knew Jesus was on His way to a celebrate a feast in Jerusalem, they rejected Him and wouldn't even give Him a place to stay. They hated the Jews so much that it offended them Jesus was planning to go worship in Jerusalem.

These were people who already acknowledged Jesus as the Messiah! They were willing to accept Jesus as God's anointed Savior, but they were unable to overcome their religious prejudice against the Jewish worship, so when Jesus identified Himself with the Jews in Jerusalem, they rejected Him. They didn't snub Jesus due to ignorance—they knew He was sent by God—they rejected Him because He was associating with a group of people they didn't like. They intentionally rejected God's anointed Savior because they couldn't get over their racial and religious hatred.

The Samaritans' rejection of Jesus was much worse than anything the army captains did to Elijah in the Old Testament story. The army captains were just obeying orders by trying to bring Elijah to King Ahaziah, but the Samaritans were rejecting the Messiah. When the disciples saw how the Samaritans were acting, they asked Jesus,

> *"...Lord, wilt thou that we command fire to come down from heaven, and consume them, even as [Elijah] did?"*
>
> *Luke 9:54*

The disciples wanted to imitate Elijah by calling down fire to kill the Samaritans, and you could argue that what the Samaritans had done was more deserving of judgment than anything the soldiers did. Yet Jesus reproached the disciples.

> *But he turned, and rebuked them, and said, Ye know not what manner of spirit ye are of. For the Son of man is not come to destroy men's lives, but to save them. And they went to another village.*

> *Luke 9:55–56*

Someone who looks at this casually might think God was being inconsistent, but the difference here is actually the difference between the Old Covenant and the New Covenant. Prior to the Law being given through Moses, which was approximately two thousand years *after* the fall of Adam and Eve, God wasn't holding people responsible for their sin (Romans 5:13). He was dealing with people in mercy and grace, but people began to take God's lack of punishment as an indication that He didn't care whether they lived a holy life or not. They didn't understand that even though God wasn't punishing sin, Satan was taking advantage of sinful actions and corrupting the whole human race. So God had to restrain sin. He had to get people to turn away from sin and the damage it was causing.

Before the Law, God wasn't punishing sin. For example, He actually protected the first murderer (Genesis 4). After Cain killed Abel, God set a mark on Cain to protect him from any vigilante-style attempts to exact justice by taking his life. God didn't approve of the murder Cain committed; it was wrong, and it had consequences, but God didn't punish Cain for his sinful action. God's grace toward Cain stands in sharp contrast to the punishment exacted upon the first person to violate the Law—a man who was picking up sticks on the Sabbath to make a fire (Numbers 15:32-36). The difference in God's reaction to these sins was that prior to the giving of the Law, God wasn't holding people accountable for their sin (Romans 5:13); He was dealing with people in grace.

The way God turned people away from sin under the Old Covenant law was by bringing judgment on the sin and using punishment. When the Law was given, it held people accountable for sin. The Law made people realize that God wasn't indifferent to the way they were acting. It revealed God's standard of righteousness, and it made the Israelites fearful of God's wrath against sin. As a result, they turned away from sin. So the law limited the amount of sin, but it also had the effect of making people feel guilty and unworthy. The Law was part of God's plan for redemption, but it was only a temporary measure put in place until Jesus should come.

> But before faith came, we were kept under the law, shut up unto the faith which should afterwards be revealed. Wherefore the law was our schoolmaster to bring us unto Christ, that we might be justified by faith. But after that faith is come, we are no longer under a schoolmaster.
>
> *Galatians 3:23-25*

Just as the giving of the Law brought judgment for sin, the sacrifice of Jesus brought a return to grace. Now that we have been transferred to the kingdom of Christ, we're no longer under a schoolmaster (Galatians 3:24-25). Jesus Christ fulfilled the Law and God isn't imputing our sins against us any longer (2 Corinthians 5:19). Under the Old Covenant, Elijah called down fire from heaven and it consumed 102 soldiers, but Jesus rebuked His disciples for wanting to do the same thing because He was ushering in a transition to the New Covenant of grace.

I believe that if Jesus had been on earth in His physical body when Elijah was calling fire down out of heaven, Jesus would have rebuked Elijah. Elijah got away with calling down fire because he was under the ministry of the Law, which was holding men's sins against them, but it was never the true nature of God to deal with people that way. It's the way He had to deal with people to restrain sin and rein us in, but it was only a temporary way of dealing with humanity. Now that grace has come through Jesus, we're no longer under the Law.

Under the Old Covenant, there were very harsh punishments for sin. The Lord often commanded the Israelites to kill all the men, women, children and even the animals when they conquered other nations (Joshua 6:17-21; 10:40; 11:11-14). There was even a commandment to kill your own children if they were persistently stubborn and rebellious (Deuteronomy 21:18-21). This was because they couldn't be cured or healed, so they were taken out of society; in much the same way that doctors cut out a cancerous tumor to save the rest of the body. It wasn't possible for anyone to be born again, and God didn't want foreign peoples infecting the children of Israel with demonic beliefs or behavior.

But under our new and better covenant (Hebrews 8:6, 13), we don't kill our rebellious children or people who are committing ungodly acts because they can be born again and changed. Praise God for the vast change that Jesus made!

Under the Old Covenant, God's judgment against evil was mercy to the rest of the body, but under the New Covenant, we can be delivered from evil. There is no need to judge individuals in order to save the rest of society. Today, we minister the love of God to anyone who is caught up in sin and we share the Good News about Jesus Christ. This difference should help us understand the harshness of the Old Testament, and why we now have a better covenant through Jesus.

Some make the mistake of thinking that the transformation in how God has related to mankind over time reflects some sort of conversion in God, which isn't true. God declares, "I am the Lord, I change not" (Malachi 3:6), and Jesus Christ is "the same yesterday, today, and forever" (Hebrews 13:8). God hasn't changed, we have—and the way He relates to us under the New Covenant has changed as a result.

> *Wherefore henceforth know we no man after the flesh: yea, though we have known Christ after the flesh, yet now henceforth know we him no more.*
>
> *2 Corinthians 5:16*

At first, the disciples related to Christ through His physical presence and attributes, but now that He has risen from the dead and ascended into heaven, we relate to Him through the Holy

Spirit. In the same way, we shouldn't look at ourselves only from a physical perspective. We have a spiritual identity that completely changed when we were born again, and we need to know who we are in the spirit—the part of us that is created new in the image of Christ.

> *Therefore if any man be in Christ, he is a new creature: old things are passed away; behold, all things are become new.*
>
> *2 Corinthians 5:17*

This is a startling statement! When you are in Christ, old things have passed away and *all* things have become new. Not some things, but all things—and they aren't in the process of transforming into something new, they *are* new.

A lot of people struggle with this scripture because they don't feel completely new, and they don't see anything new in themselves. They say, "I still get angry. I still have some of the same bad habits. I feel like I'm getting better, but I'm not there yet." They struggle with accepting the idea that they are already new because they don't understand that this scripture isn't talking about your physical body or your personality. Getting born again doesn't cause obesity to disappear, and it doesn't automatically change your personality. The Holy Spirit can help you improve, and you can change, but it isn't automatic. Your thoughts and memories don't immediately change, but in the spirit you become a totally brand new person—instantly.

The reason you don't see a totally new person when you look in the mirror is that you are looking at your physical appearance or searching your mental and emotional makeup, but the changes in your spirit cannot be perceived by your natural senses. Your spirit is the part of you that becomes completely new. Look at how the Amplified Bible translates this scripture:

> *Therefore if any person is [ingrafted] in Christ (the Messiah) he is a new creation (a new creature altogether); the old [previous moral and spiritual condition] has passed away. Behold, the fresh and new has come!*

In your spirit, your salvation is perfect. You have been united with Christ and your spirit is as perfect, pure, and holy as it ever will be. The moment you are born again, your spirit is transformed into the new creation you will be for all of eternity. Your spirit will never change. We will get new heavenly bodies, and our souls will be renewed so that we know all things even as we are known (1 Corinthians 13:12), but our spirits are changed forever the moment we get born again. The next verses say,

> *And all things are of God, who hath reconciled us to himself by Jesus Christ, and hath given to us the ministry of reconciliation; To wit, that God was in Christ, reconciling the world unto himself, not imputing their trespasses unto them; and hath committed unto us the word of reconciliation.*

> *2 Corinthians 5:18-19*

God has already—past tense—reconciled us to himself through Jesus Christ; more specifically, God was, in Christ, reconciling the sins of the entire human race. "Reconcile" is a term we don't use every day, but it just means to reestablish a close relationship between, or to settle or resolve. God took away all of the discord that sin caused and He harmonized our relationship with Him again.

This scripture also says God is not "imputing" our sins anymore, which means to attribute responsibility for. It is a term used in bookkeeping to describe charging or accrediting fees to an account. For instance, when you use a credit card to purchase something, you are really asking the seller to give you the item and charge - or impute - the fee to your account. The item isn't actually paid for until you pay off your credit card. You didn't pay for the item when you gave the seller your credit card; you just had the cost imputed to your account. If you don't believe that, just refuse to pay the credit card bill when it comes and see if they think you've already paid.

When Scripture says that God reconciled the world unto Himself, not imputing our trespasses unto us, it means that God didn't charge sin to our account. He went ahead and paid the debt for us—a balance that was impossible for us to settle—so that He could reestablish a close relationship with us.

> *For he hath made him to be sin for us, who knew no sin; that*
> *we might be made the righteousness of God in him.*
>
> *2 Corinthians 5:21*

God took the sins of all humanity and charged it to the account of Jesus, and He was also in Jesus on Calvary. God didn't just turn His head and pretend sin never happened. No, sin had a cost—death—that had to be paid (Romans 6:23). God's pure, holy, and righteous nature wouldn't allow Him to look the other way, yet He loves us and desires a relationship with us, so God decided to pay for sin Himself. Sin was still imputed, but instead of charging us, God charged it to His Son.

Going back to the credit card illustration, imagine if you were to roll a cartload of computer gear to the checkout in an electronics store and just as you are about to be charged, someone steps up and says, "Let me get that for you," and puts it all on his credit card. That's very different from the store clerk saying to you, "Don't worry about it. Everything is free today." The items aren't free—someone has to pay for them. Similarly, I give away a lot of my materials for free, but it isn't because I have unlimited resources. Everything we give away has a cost; it's just that we absorb the expense. We pay the cost to help those who can't afford to buy materials.

God didn't say, "Oh, let's just forget sin. Let's not impute sin anymore." No, sin had a cost that had to be paid—a price we couldn't possibly pay—so God charged it to His own account. He put all of our sin upon his Son, the Lord Jesus. He made Jesus, who never sinned, become sin for us, and He took the sin of the entire human race (2 Corinthians 5:21). The apostle John wrote,

> *And he is the propitiation for our sins: and not for ours only, but also for the sins of the whole world.*
>
> *1 John 2:2*

Jesus didn't just die for a select number of people who would later accept Him. No, Jesus paid for the sins of the whole world, even the people who reject Him. Hitler's sins, for example, were paid for—Jesus took the murder of six million Jews and the responsibility for a World War upon Himself. Jesus suffered shame, hurt, and degradation on Hitler's behalf. All of that evil was charged to Jesus. Jesus suffered all of the humiliation and depression that results from sin for every person who has ever lived—billions and billions of people.

That doesn't mean Hitler was saved. Because, as far as we know, Hitler didn't accept the salvation that Jesus provided. All of his actions indicate he was in rebellion towards the Lord and in union with the devil. We have to humble ourselves and make Jesus our Lord (Romans 10:9) for what He did for us to be credited to our account.

Once you truly understand the significance of Jesus' sacrifice, then you can understand why God dealt with people differently under the New Covenant than He did under the Old Covenant. God didn't change—God never changes—but the atoning sacrifice of Jesus changed everything. Under the Old Covenant, the payment for sin had not been made and people bore their own sins. People bore the wrath and the punishment of God.

You can find a limited amount of mercy under the Old Covenant, but only to the degree that people understood God's grace nature and operated in it. King David is a good example: when he committed adultery with Bathsheba, according to the Old Testament law, he should have been stoned to death. Yet God showed him mercy because David understood the true nature of

God. In a sense, David was able to reach into the future by faith and appropriate some of the grace that we live under in the New Covenant. You can see this reflected in the psalm David wrote when he said, "Against thee, thee only, have I sinned and done this evil in thy sight" (Psalm 51:4). David showed his understanding of God's true nature when he went on to say that he would offer a sacrifice, but he knew that sacrifice was not what God really wanted (verse 16). Under the Old Covenant, David was supposed to offer a blood sacrifice for his sin, but by his own admission, he knew it wasn't what God really wanted. David broke free from the Old Testament system and offered the sacrifice of a contrite heart.

Instead of David being killed in the way the Law prescribed, God showed him mercy. But we also see the Old Covenant punishment for sin in how the child who was born to Bathsheba was killed in judgment. We don't see that kind of judgment under the New Covenant. God has always desired to relate to us by grace, but He couldn't under the Old Covenant because of humanity's hardness of heart. Fortunately, the debt of sin has been paid now and God is free to be just and merciful.

Jesus coming to this earth made a pivotal difference in the way God deals with mankind. Without the sacrifice of Jesus, humanity would still be living under God's wrath against sin. Instead, God poured out all of His wrath against sin on Jesus (John 12:32). God isn't judging our sin now because the judgment for all sin, for all time, was put on Jesus.

Who his own self bare our sins in his own body on the tree, that
we, being dead to sins, should live unto righteousness: by whose
stripes ye were healed.

1 Peter 2:24

Does that mean we are free to go live however we want? Of course not. Sin has negative consequences that are purely natural, and it gives Satan an inroad into our individual lives and into our society (Romans 6:16). When our societies promote ungodly principles and make morality a completely private issue, then it gives Satan an opportunity to destroy nations (Proverbs 14:34). Society cannot continue to seek the immorality it promotes and succeed in the long run, but the consequences of sin are not a punishment from God.

Chapter Eight
What About Suffering?

C ertain Bible verses dealing with suffering have frequently been misinterpreted and are sometimes used to suggest that God uses suffering to teach us a lesson or to help us grow spiritually. I believe those interpretations are harmful and cause people to have a wrong understanding of God's true nature. One of the frequently misinterpreted scriptures says,

> *My brethren, count it all joy when ye fall into divers temptations; Knowing this, that the trying of your faith worketh patience. But let patience have her perfect work, that ye may be perfect and entire, wanting nothing.*

> *James 1:2–4*

These verses have been used by many to imply that praying for patience means God will put trials and temptations in our way in order to teach us patience. We've all heard someone say, "Be careful what you pray for," as if problems are actually the work of God intended to bring us to maturity. The church I grew up in talked about problems as "heavenly sandpaper" that rubbed off all of our rough edges and made us better people.

145

Let me make an obvious statement: If suffering and problems were what make you a better person, then the people who have suffered the most should be the holiest, most godly people on earth—but that isn't the case. In fact, the opposite is usually true. The people who have suffered the most are often bitter, angry people whose lives are a mess. It simply is not an observable truth to say that suffering produces holiness.

On the other hand, it is true to say that when you respond to hardship by trusting in God, it brings to the surface things God has placed on the inside of you. As you depend on God's strength, you become stronger in your faith—but the hardships aren't what make you better. What makes you stronger is exercising your faith in God and trusting in Him. The strength comes through the improvement of your relationship with God as you seek Him, so hardship might cause you to seek God, but suffering doesn't make you a better person.

The Vietnam War was a trying situation on my faith, and I came out of it much stronger than when I went in—but God didn't organize the war to make me holy. God didn't have people criticize me for my stance on Christianity or put me in a bunker that was wallpapered with pictures of nude women. The Lord didn't do those things to make me stronger, but I did become stronger through those trials because I kept my faith and trust in God.

When I was drafted into the Army, they taught me how to fire a rifle, how to throw grenades, plant mines, and defend myself in hand-to-hand combat. The Army spent six months training me to fight in a war, and then they sent me to Vietnam. But training and information are not equal to experience. After I had been in Vietnam for a short period of time, I learned to be wary of new recruits who had just arrived in country because they were dangerous. Officers were particularly dangerous because they could arrive straight from school—with no combat experience—and start ordering people around.

I remember being on bunker guard one night with a brand new guy and a bunch of other soldiers who had been in Vietnam for a while. We were sitting around eating our C-rations and the new guy said, "Can I throw a hand grenade? Can I fire my rifle?" On the fire support base I was at, we did those things all the time; it was a normal part of pulling bunker guard. We would just randomly fire outside the perimeter to deter the enemy from sneaking up on us. The new guy was all excited to blow some stuff up, so we told him to go ahead. He pulled the pin on a grenade, and as he did, the grenade came out of his hand and bounced down between my feet. The way we all scattered you'd have thought the grenade exploded, but it didn't. Luckily, it was a new style of grenade with an extra safety on it. The point is that the new guy was dangerous because he had knowledge but lacked experience.

Becoming a good soldier involves putting into practice all of the things you learn through training, so you do become a better soldier after you have engaged in combat. You learn things through experience that you can't learn from a book. But it would be insane to embrace the enemy when he attacks you, as if his purpose is to make you a better soldier. The enemy isn't there to make you better—he's there to kill you. Only by resisting the enemy and overcoming him will you live through the attack and become a better soldier.

Likewise, God doesn't send problems into your life to make you a better person—the enemy tries to create problems in order to cause suffering. It would be crazy to embrace trials and tribulations as if they are good things. Afflictions and persecutions come to steal the Word of God out of your heart (Mark 4:17). They come to discourage you and to undermine your faith. Sickness comes to defeat you. Financial problems come to cause anxiety and to limit what you can do for the kingdom of God. To embrace those problems as if they are sent by God to make you a better person is crazy. But if, through faith, you continue to trust in God's promises and resist the enemy, then you will overcome the challenges and prosper in spite of them.

Going through hardship and using your faith in God is going to make you a stronger Christian on the other side, but I am not encouraging anybody to accept hardship as a blessing from God. Hardship is not a blessing. It's a curse from the enemy. You are only made stronger through hardship by resisting it and standing in faith.

Let no man say when he is tempted, I am tempted of God: for God cannot be tempted with evil, neither tempteth he any man: But every man is tempted, when he is drawn away of his own lust, and enticed.

James 1:13-14

What About Suffering?

Scripture couldn't be any clearer in saying that suffering and temptation are not from God, yet many religious traditions continue to blame God. The foundation of this teaching on Christian Philosophy is the apostle Paul's warning for us not to be spoiled through philosophy (Colossians 2:8). This teaching that God sends hardships to make us better is a religious tradition that has spoiled untold numbers of Christians. They believe God is orchestrating the problems in their lives, and using suffering for some redemptive purpose. That attitude will make you passive because it takes away your desire to resist problems.

If it was God's will for you to have cancer, why would you go to the doctor and try to get out of His will? If God wants you to be sick, why would you fight against Him by trying to get better? The more sincere your desire to please God, the more likely you are to give up in the face of hardship if you believe God is behind your problems. Believing God will send problems into our lives is a false teaching that has kept us from having a positive relationship with Him. It's impossible to really trust someone and have a healthy relationship with them if you are constantly wondering whether they might hurt you—even if they are supposedly doing it for your own good.

What would you think of me if I were personally responsible for every baby born with a deformity or disability? How much would you like me if you knew that I was responsible for every death, disease, hardship, and tragedy in the world? Would you want to be my friend or spend any time with me? Who in their right mind would want to get close to me if having a relationship with me might mean that I would "bless" you with some incurable disease or kill the people you love most? I can guarantee you that if I were guilty of all the things people are blaming God for, society would lock me up and throw away the key.

Just as Satan convinced Adam and Eve that the Lord wasn't all good, but that He had withheld His best from them, so religion (which is the devil's creation) has put forth the lie that the Lord is responsible for all the bad things in our lives. That just isn't so.

Many people have misunderstood the true nature of God, and they are proclaiming that nothing happens without God's permission. Therefore, they say, He must be responsible for all of the suffering in our world. Then they try to defend their position by saying God is sending the evil for our own good. It's a total misrepresentation of who God is and how He relates to us.

I know a number of people who are running from God because they think He is responsible for the evil in the world. One of their main arguments is, "How could a good God allow all of this to happen?" But God is not the source of the suffering in our world. God does not tempt us with hardship, there is no shadow of evil in Him, and He only blesses us with good things.

> *Do not err, my beloved brethren. Every good gift and every perfect gift is from above, and cometh down from the Father of lights, with whom is no variableness, neither shadow of turning.*
>
> *James 1:16–17*

"Do not err" is another way of saying, "Unless you believe what I'm saying, you're wrong." The simplest Christian philosophy you can have is to know that if something is good, then it's from God; if it's bad, then it's from the devil. Only good and perfect gifts come down from our Heavenly Father— sickness, hardship, and suffering are not good and perfect gifts.

The goodness of God has to be the trump card against all arguments and circumstances in your life. No matter what is going on, you have to know absolutely that God is a good God. The moment someone starts trying to tell you that God gave you a sickness or put hardship in your life, the absolute certainty of God's goodness should rise up within you and immediately reject what they are saying.

Unfortunately, a lot of religious teaching portrays God in a very bad light. These teachers are trying to say God is dangling people over hell by a thin thread—that He is angry with us, and He is out to get us. I've even heard people say that if you don't tithe, God is going to punish you by taking the money from you in doctors' bills. Other preachers say that if you leave their church, you are departing from God's will, and the wrath of God will descend on you by destroying your family, contracting some disease, or some other tragedy. A lot of those teachers are trying to drive people to God through fear of punishment, but Scripture says it is the goodness of God that leads men to repentance (Romans 2:4). We should be telling people about the extravagant goodness of God, not threatening them.

God doesn't send problems into your life, but if you believe He does, then it is going to be hard for you to believe that He is truly good. It is easy to say God is a good God in theory, but if you don't really believe it, then your relationship is going to be hindered. Every time someone you love becomes ill or tragedy strikes, it is going to chip away at your resolve that God only wants good things for you. Look at this scripture:

> *But after that the kindness and love of God our Saviour toward man appeared, Not by works of righteousness which we have done, but according to his mercy he saved us, by the washing of regeneration, and renewing of the Holy Ghost; Which he shed on us abundantly through Jesus Christ our Saviour.*

> *Titus 3:4-6*

God's kindness and love toward us have nothing to do with any righteousness on our part. Too many people are preaching that you have to earn God's favor, and that He is only good toward us when we deserve it, but that isn't true. If you think you have to earn God's love, then you will never believe God is good because your conscience will always condemn you. It doesn't matter how holy you live, you are always going to fall short of God's standard of holiness, which will leave you feeling separated from God. Our righteousness comes from God, so if you are depending on your own righteousness to make you feel worthy of God's love, then you are never going to feel worthy.

The summer before Oral Roberts died, I was privileged to have the opportunity to meet with him in his home. While I was there, people were asking him questions about all of the things God had done in his life. Oral's response was that he didn't understand how or why God had used him. He said that there was nothing special about him, except that God touched his life. The same thing is true of every Christian.

When I look at all of the things God has done for me, I am overwhelmed by His goodness. God has sought after me more than I have searched for Him. My life could have turned out a lot differently than it has if it wasn't for the goodness of God. For instance, one of my sons was dead for five hours. My wife Jamie and I prayed that God would raise him from the dead, and out of His mercy and love, God did raise him back to life, but it wasn't because of anything I deserved. I now have a granddaughter I wouldn't have if it wasn't for the goodness of God.

My father died when I was 12 years old—and he was only 54 at the time. I don't believe it was God's will for him to die. I have never believed that God took my father, even though my pastor told me that he died because God needed him in heaven. It wasn't God's fault that my father died, but God was with me and He blessed me through the ordeal. I remember the Sunday morning our pastor came to our house to talk to my brother and me about our father's death. Immediately, a supernatural peace of God came over me and the Lord brought to my remembrance a scripture from Psalm 27: "When my father and my mother forsake me, then the LORD will take me up" (v. 10). From that moment on, God took me up. He became my Father and my best friend. Even though it wasn't God's will for my father to die, I can look back and see the goodness of God blessing me through that experience.

I can't tell you how many aspects of my life have been affected by the goodness of God. I believe that we can all look back on our lives and see how God worked to bless us, despite tragedy we may have endured. I remember the Holy Spirit giving me supernatural knowledge about a woman at one of my meetings who had suffered a history of abuse. Terrible things had been done to her, but God had saved her life. He delivered her from the hands of the abusers whose plan was to kill her. Through the gifts of the Holy Spirit, I began to help her see that God had blessed her. She had a husband and a wonderful family, and God had been good to her. She went from being focused on the horrors of the abuse, to seeing how God had intervened in her life with mercy and love. In the same way, each one of us can see the goodness of God in our lives, even if we have suffered tragedy.

> *And we know that all things work together for good to them that love God, to them who are the called according to his purpose.*

> *Romans 8:28*

Most people have heard this scripture used as a blanket statement to convey that whatever happens must be God's will—that God works all things together for good, so there must be some purpose behind the tragedies in our lives. But just because God can bring good out of tragedy doesn't mean He caused the tragedy or wants us to endure suffering. It's true that exercising our faith through trials causes us to emerge stronger on the other side, but this verse does not say that God causes everything that happens in our lives.

God works all things together for good, but He doesn't cause all things—and things don't work together for good for *every person*. It's pretty obvious when you look around that not everything that happens ultimately works out for good. Some people have tragic lives that end in bitterness, anger, and destitution. A life of destructive choices often adds up to a disastrous ending, so there are some qualifications on exactly how "all things work together for good."

This scripture doesn't say that all things end well for all people; it says that things work together for good for *"those who love God."* That single qualification dramatically limits the number of people this scripture applies to because the majority of people do not love God.

I can remember being at a Full Gospel Businessmen's meeting a long time ago when the speaker used this scripture to talk about God working everything together for good. He had just come from conducting the funeral of a teenage boy and girl who died in a vehicle accident. They had been drinking and were speeding down the roadway in a rainstorm. The car went into a turn too fast, the driver lost control, and they crashed into a telephone pole—killing both of them. Neither of them was known to be Christian, so as far as we know they didn't go straight to the arms of Jesus—they went to eternal punishment. Clearly, there was nothing good about the accident, and if they did end up in hell, then zero redemptive value came out of it.

Yet this minister used Romans 8:28 to say that God had a purpose in this tragedy and it was working together for good. That's not right. God didn't do this. I'm sure the Lord convicted these teenagers that what they were doing was wrong and tried to sway them from that path. But God doesn't control us like pawns. We have free will and He won't force us to make the right choices.

It should be clear that good doesn't come out of every situation for every person. If you don't love God, then things aren't necessarily going to work together for good. The reason I'm stressing this point is because if you believe that God controls every single thing that happens, then you are going to get the impression that God isn't a good God. If you think God caused those two kids to get drunk and drive too fast on a wet road and killed them and sent them to hell, then you aren't going to believe God is a good God.

Some people can see that God doesn't cause suffering, but they think He "allows" it to happen, but Scripture says that God reveals Himself "…against all ungodliness and unrighteousness of men" (Romans 1:18). In the case of the two teenagers who died in the car accident, I believe that God gave them an intuitive knowledge of right and wrong and convicted them that what they were doing was wrong. I believe God spoke to them hundreds of times before they crashed the car and died—not just on the night of the accident, but in all the years leading up to it. God didn't "allow" the accident to happen, in the sense that He didn't intervene in any way to stop it. It's more like there was a mountain of obstacles that God put in their way, but they persisted and climbed over all of the things God was doing to save them.

Don't we all want the best for our children? Scripture says that if we, being the imperfect and sinful people that we are, can wish good for our children, then how much more will our Heavenly Father do good for us when we ask Him (Matthew 7:9-11). Anyone who goes to hell has to ignore the thousands and thousands of times God has tried to convict them and draw them into His love. Going to hell isn't a one-time decision; it is the result of rejecting God countless times. Our God is a good God, and He desires good things for us—even more than we desire good for our children.

Not only does the scripture in the book of Romans say that things work together for good for those who love God, it also says that it does so for "…them who are the called according to his purpose" (Romans 8:28). God's purposes are redemptive. The Bible says that Jesus came to earth to destroy the works of the devil (1 John 3:8), so to be called according to His purpose means that you are resisting the works of the devil (James 4:7). If you are rebelling against God and chasing sin, then the tragedy that occurs in your life is not necessarily going to work together for good.

Another qualification of the promise found in Romans 8:28 appears in the verses just previous to it. Romans 8:28 begins, "And we know that all things work together for good…" *And* is a conjunction linking the statement about good to the previous sentences, which talk about the Holy Spirit making intercession through us. The Holy Spirit doesn't pray without you, but when you start to pray, the Holy Spirit comes alongside you and pleads your cause. When you have that kind of Spirit-led intercession working in your life, then things are going to work together for good.

So we see there are three major qualifications on things working together for good: you have to love God, you have to be resisting the works of the devil, and you have to pray—allowing the Holy Spirit to help you make intercession. Scripture does not say God is orchestrating everything that happens in our lives, and if we aren't trying to meet those three qualifications, then everything isn't necessarily going to work together for good.

God is not the cause of all the evil in our world. He isn't killing people because He loves them so much. God is a good God. His plans for your life are peace and victory (Jeremiah 29:11), but God's will doesn't come to pass automatically; you have to cooperate with Him. Once you believe that God is only good, your faith will abound and you will see better results in your life. You can cooperate with God, and all things *will* work together for good.

A lot of negative things happen in life: people we love die, children get sick, jobs are lost, and tragedy strikes when we least expect it. It's easy to look at the circumstances in life and wonder why our all-powerful God doesn't prevent suffering, which can then lead you to think that God is responsible for that suffering, but Scripture reveals that God has nothing to do with evil.

When God created the heavens and the earth, everything was perfect. God told Adam not to eat of the tree of the knowledge of good and evil because in the day he did, he would die. Adam rejected God's instructions and the result was that sin entered creation. Every one of us has leaned unto our own understanding rather than depending on God, and our rebellion is what has released evil on earth. Satan is the cause of suffering. He roams around seeking whom he may devour; he steals, kills, and destroys (1 Peter 5:8 and John 10:10). God is not the source of the tragedy in our lives!

The Bible is full of proof that God is a good God. The ultimate testimony is that Jesus came to this earth and suffered, not only on the cross, but also by humbling Himself and taking on human form for 33 years. Jesus suffered by being confined to a physical human body when he was God. Solomon said, "The heaven and heaven of heavens cannot contain thee; how much less this house that I have [built]?" (1 Kings 8:27). God is infinite—even the universe can't contain Him—yet He limited Himself to a physical body. He was despised and rejected by men, and He ultimately took the punishment for our sins. If God loved you enough to suffer and die for you, He loves you enough to do anything for you.

> *Let them shout for joy, and be glad, that favour my righteous cause: yea, let them say continually, Let the LORD be magnified, which hath pleasure in the prosperity of his servant.*
>
> *Psalm 35:27*

God is pleased when you prosper. He wants to see you succeed. Nobody is pulling for you more than God is, which might not be what you are used to hearing, but it's the message the Bible teaches. God is love (1 John 4:7-8). God doesn't just love some people or have a little love for all. He *is* love.

> *In this was manifested the love of God toward us, because that God sent his only begotten Son into the world, that we might live through him. Herein is love, not that we loved God, but that he loved us, and sent his Son to be the propitiation for our sins.*
>
> 1 John 4:9-10

God showed us His love by sending Jesus. I am convinced that if you focus on God sending Jesus to earth, instead of just hearing the words, you will experience the fruit of God's peace and joy. If God's love isn't impacting you or how you feel about life, then take time to be still and meditate on this truth that God showed His love for us by sending His Son. God's love will be revealed to you when you focus on the fact that Jesus came to earth to become the payment for our sin.

Salvation isn't about us loving God first and then, because we initiate relationship with Him, God extends love to us in return. God's loving nature is revealed in that He reached out to us while we were rejecting Him. Christ died for us while we were still living in sin.

What About Suffering?

But God commendeth his love towards us, in that, while we were yet sinners, Christ died for us.

Romans 5:8

God has already given you His Son, why wouldn't He give you joy, peace, health, and prosperity (Romans 8:32)? It would be totally inconsistent for me to be willing to die for you, but unwilling to give you some money. God not only has the ability to heal and prosper us, *He desires to do it*. Faith works by love, and if we trust and believe in God's love—by focusing on what He has already done for us—our faith will rise.

Jesus didn't have to suffer death on a cross, He chose to. He could have called down an army of angels, but He humbly submitted to a humiliating death instead (Matthew 26:53). Jesus allowed the scribes and Pharisees to mock Him. They spit in His face, slapped Him, insulted Him, beat Him, and finally killed Him. Jesus took all of that because He loved us and wanted to save us.

The life, death, and resurrection of Jesus were a physical manifestation of God's love pursuing us, and when Jesus ascended into heaven, He gave us the Holy Spirit to continue His ministry on earth until He returns. The Holy Spirit is our Teacher and Helper. He leads us into all truth, and He is the eyes of the Lord that search the whole earth, as He seeks to show Himself strong on behalf of those who love God (2 Chronicles 16:9).

The Lord is looking for you. He isn't hiding from you. You don't have to pursue Him. You just need to slow down and unplug from the distractions of the world for a little bit. You can't make a connection with God in the three minutes between your two favorite television shows. You need to find time to be still and know God (Psalm 46:10). I'm not just referring to physical stillness, but stillness in your mind, which just means not being completely occupied with other thoughts. God wants to reveal His love for you more than you desire to know it, but He isn't going to force His way into your life. You have to take time and give God the opportunity to show you His love.

> *Behold, I stand at the door, and knock: if any man hear my voice, and open the door, I will come in to him, and will sup with him, and he with me.*

Revelation 3:20

This verse has been used to talk about being born again—which isn't wrong—but this letter was written to Christians. Jesus was saying this to people who were already born again. He is asking you to let Him into your life. Will you give Him your attention? Will you unplug from the distractions of life that keep you from hearing the voice of God and simply focus on His voice? The results of knowing God's love are tremendous. It is worth sacrificing a little entertainment in front of the television to sit quietly in the presence of the Lord.

I can't tell you how many people come to me in fear of the circumstances in their lives. They are fearful over the future, the economy, kids, relationships, health, and all kinds of other things. A lot of people today are living in fear, but God's love will push the fear out of your life. Scripture says that there is no fear in love

(1 John 4:18). When you spend time in the presence of God, the experience of His love kills your fears. It is impossible for fear to thrive where God's love dwells.

During the Vietnam War, I visited a forward fire support base that was overrun by the enemy just hours after I left. Before I was evacuated by helicopter, I remember seeing the muzzle flashes from the rifle fire of the enemy as they charged up the hill toward our position, but I wasn't afraid. I was worshipping God. I was actually thinking, *Lord, today could be the day I come to meet You!* I had supernatural compassion for the people who were rushing to kill me. I had no fear of dying. All I experienced was love and excitement about the possibility of going to be with the Lord.

Once you know God and understand how good He is, you can become like the apostle Paul, who said: "For to me to live is Christ, and to die is gain" (Philippians 1:21). This is normal Christianity. It sounds a little extreme by the world's standards, but this is the attitude we should have.

The suffering of this life is not worthy of being compared with the glory that will be revealed in us (Romans 8:18). We have something so awesome prepared for us in the presence of God that we won't give a second thought to the heartache and rejection we experienced in this life. Nobody in heaven is grieving over the things that happened to them during their lives on earth. If you were to really think about this, you wouldn't have any fear of poverty, sickness, or failure. Whatever this world has to throw at you, God has something greater in store.

God has been misrepresented as causing the tragedy in our world, and I believe that is the number one reason people are not seeking relationship with Him. If you think God is causing the problems in your life, then you'll want to keep Him at arm's length—even if you are a Christian. It's a natural response to try to avoid people and situations that might hurt you. But God isn't causing the suffering in our world. In fact, God has nothing to do with it.

God loves you, and He desires good things for you, but experiencing the love of God passes mere knowledge about His love (Ephesians 3:19). Once you understand how good God is and begin having a real relationship with Him, you open yourself to receiving His love and being filled with all the fullness of God. The blessings of God will come upon you and overtake you, and it will cause everything to work out for good in your life.

Part II
Chapter 9
Social Issues: Christians Must Speak Up

Before we start looking at the biblical perspective on social issues and how to apply our Christian philosophy, I want to establish my right as a minister to discuss current affairs. I feel like this is necessary because many people have adopted the attitude that ministers can say all they want—as long as they stay in church. Much of society thinks that Christianity should be a privately held conviction that never gets talked about publicly.

In America, the notion of "separation of church and state" has been misunderstood and misapplied. Contrary to popular belief, the phrase does not appear anywhere in Constitution of the United States, but was used in a private letter written by Thomas Jefferson in reference to state-sponsored religion. He was against the government mandating the religion of its citizens—his statement had nothing to do with Christianity being totally removed from the public arena. There is a big difference between the two.

Critics have used the phrase "separation of church and state" to beat Christians into retreat. Unbelievers want us to withdraw into the walls of church buildings and not speak out on moral issues, but you can't separate Christianity from current affairs. The very notion of worldview means that your life is influenced—if not determined—by what you believe. You cannot compartmentalize your life into a separation of religious conviction and political affiliation. Who you are, what you believe, and how you act in everyday life are inseparable. Jesus said that a house divided won't stand for long (Mark 3:25), so you're headed for trouble when you try to divide your life into parts that relate to God and parts that don't.

Christians have every right to speak out on current affairs because the stance you take on social issues is as relevant to your relationship with God as church affairs. If your position on social issues is in opposition to God's revealed will, then you are creating a division in yourself that will, at the very least, make you insensitive to God's leading. The Bible has a lot to say about moral issues in society, and ministers need to talk about morality so Christians understand the biblical perspective.

One reason ungodliness is advancing in our culture is that a lot of Christians have retreated from the public forum. They have been intimidated into silence, but we shouldn't draw back from those who oppose God. Scripture says,

> *Thou shalt not hate thy brother in thine heart: thou shalt in any wise rebuke thy neighbour, and not suffer sin upon him. Thou shalt not avenge, nor bear any grudge against the children of thy people, but thou shalt love thy neighbour as thyself: I am the* LORD.

Leviticus 19:17–18

Jesus quoted this passage when He said that the two greatest commandments are to love God, and to love your neighbor as yourself (Matthew 22:37-40). This passage in Leviticus says that loving your neighbor can mean letting them know when they are wrong, by not allowing them to live in sin ignorantly. Actually, the command to rebuke your neighbor is given as the opposite of hating your neighbor in your heart—by allowing them to live in sin without any reproach. Remaining silent while the world around you revels in sin isn't loving your neighbor; it's esteeming yourself above your neighbor.

It's true that the moment you speak out against immorality, people who disagree with you are going to say things to try to shut you up, like calling you intolerant or close-minded, but we can't let criticism and persecution keep us from speaking the truth in love. Despite what some think, morality isn't relative to the circumstances. Certain things are always wrong, and Christians should speak out against those things. We can't keep quiet about immorality because we are afraid of criticism.

I have received a lot of criticism over the years for speaking out on social issues. My television program has been removed from television stations, and the broadcasting channel in one country has edited out material they considered provocative. They do this not because I'm saying mean or offensive things, but because some biblical positions are not considered politically correct enough to mention on television. I don't like rejection and criticism, but I'm not going to stop speaking the truth just because some people don't want to hear it.

Sometimes loving your neighbors means telling them when they are wrong, so it isn't hate speech to tell someone the truth. The Word says, "Thou shalt not hate thy brother in thine heart: thou shalt in any wise rebuke thy neighbor, and not suffer sin upon him." When you know something is wrong, but refuse to talk about it because you don't want to be criticized, then your behavior shows hate toward the person who is engaged in wrongdoing.

I believe it is especially important for ministers to speak out on moral issues because a lot of Christians honestly don't know what the Word of God says about some of the things happening today. Many Christians have been listening to worldly perspectives for so long that they have taken on worldly attitudes. Their moral compass is completely out of whack.

I'm going to give you the scriptural perspective on current social issues such as evolution, abortion, and homosexuality, but I'm also going to discuss the natural evidence that supports those biblical positions. I'm satisfied just knowing what the Word of God says, but I know many Christians who have adopted worldly viewpoints are going to want evidence from other sources, so I'm going to present the natural evidence. All of this is done to help you understand how to apply your Christian philosophy to issues you face in daily life.

The issues I will discuss are subjects about which I believe many Christians are confused. My hope is that you will discover truths you aren't aware of, and it will reinforce your trust in the Word of God. With God there is forgiveness, and our job as Christians is to minister love to people lost in sin, so my motivation for speaking out against immorality is not to hurt anyone. I am not against sinners—but I am against sin, and the pain it causes. This should be your motivation for applying Christian philosophy in your life as well.

I live in the mountains of Colorado, and a number of years ago I was driving home on a foggy night with really poor visibility. A car passed me just as I was going into a sharp turn, and almost as soon as the car pulled in front of me, its brake lights came on and the car jerked violently. I immediately slammed on my brakes and swerved right to avoid hitting the car. I ended up stopping on the shoulder of the road right beside the other car, which had struck a horse. The car was seriously damaged as a result of the collision, and it was sitting in the middle of the road.

As I sat there wondering what to do, a large sport utility vehicle came around the corner behind me and had to swerve to avoid the car stuck in the middle of the road. As it swerved, the SUV ran over the horse carcass and the driver of the SUV was also injured.

At that point, both lanes of the curve were blocked on a dark foggy night, and people were driving 60 mph heading into the curve. I knew more people were going to get hurt if I didn't do something to warn the oncoming traffic. I didn't have a flashlight or anything, so the only thing I could do was stand out in the road and try to flag people down. The problem was it was so foggy that drivers couldn't see me until they were so close it was dangerous.

I was jumping out in front of cars going 60 mph, and they were slamming on their brakes and skidding all over the road.

A couple of people pulled over and got out of their vehicles to cuss me out. I'm sure they were pretty ticked off at me for scaring them, but I guarantee you that as soon as they came around the next corner and saw the wreck, they realized I was trying to help them. It was better for them to dodge a pedestrian attempting to slow them down, than to go full speed around the corner and plow into another vehicle.

It took the police thirty minutes to arrive at the accident and take control of the traffic. I don't know how many people I stopped from speeding around the corner and getting into an accident, ujikbut it was a lot. People could have been killed. I risked bodily injury and criticism, but it was the right thing to do. It would have been selfish for me to get myself to safety and then stand by and watch car after car speed around the corner and crash into each other—just because I didn't want to get involved or anger oncoming drivers by trying to flag them down.

I believe that speaking out on moral issues is a similar situation. The Word of God speaks against immoral behaviors because they are destructive. It would be selfish of me not to warn others of the dangers of destructive behavior just because I don't want to be criticized. I know some people are going to call me intolerant and close-minded, but I am not discussing these things to make anyone angry. I'm speaking out on social issues to save lives and prevent injury, and I'm not going to let criticism or rejection prevent me from speaking the truth in love; because I believe it is not only the right of Christians to speak out on immoral trends in society, but our duty as well.

Chapter 10

Creation vs. Evolution

D r. Richard Von Sternberg, an evolutionary biologist, is a former editor of a prominent scientific journal associated with the Smithsonian Museum of Natural History. After an article which Dr. Von Sternberg chose to publish for the journal was printed, he was immediately pressured to resign, and an investigation into his political and religious beliefs was conducted. Halfway across the country at Baylor University, science professor Robert Marks, who was approaching tenure in his position at the college, suddenly had his professional website shut down by the university and was forced to return research grant money to the school.[26]

What horrible crime did these two well-respected scientists commit that sparked such outrage and drastic action to be taken against them? They dared to mention, within their sphere of influence, an evolutionist's two most-feared words: *intelligent design.* Even the consideration of life being created instead of coming

---

[26] Nathan Frankowski, Kevin Miller, & Ben Stein. "Expelled: No Intelligence Allowed." Premise Media Corporation and Rampant Films. 2008. DVD

about as the result of random chance is considered heretical by evolutionists.

In Dr. Von Sternberg's case, he published an article by another scientist who merely suggested that intelligent design might be able to explain how life began. Those in the scientific community were so upset about the article, that Von Sternberg was thereafter labeled as an "intellectual terrorist."

As Professor Marks learned, even at some institutes of higher learning that carry a Christian label, like Baylor, being associated with any concept other than evolution can cost you your career. When the university discovered a link between Marks' research and intelligent design, they completely ostracized him. For Marks, who used his website to promote himself and his research in order to obtain grant money, it was devastating, both financially and professionally. Professor Marks was shocked by Baylor's reaction to his work. "I have never been treated like this in my thirty years of academia," he stated.[27]

Dr. Von Sternberg and Professor Marks are only two examples of the kind of treatment a person can expect to receive when going against the tide of evolution. Hundreds, if not thousands, of excellent and well-loved professors have been fired or forced to resign for simply making a comment about intelligent design in their classrooms, even in those schools that pride themselves on having "healthy debate" and a "diversity of opinions." And many scientists have found themselves blackballed from the scientific community,

---

[27] Ibid.

essentially ending their careers, because of research they've conducted that even hints at intelligent design.

But there are others—many others—who have evolved, so to speak, from believing in evolution to now believing in intelligent design or creationism, yet they do not dare to openly confess their new way of thinking. Hidden in our universities, high schools, and research labs, are ex-atheists, ex-agnostics, and ex-evolutionists who have discovered the lie behind evolution. Unfortunately, they must keep their discoveries to themselves.

So, it makes you wonder—what is it that the scientific and educational institutions are so afraid of? Why do they try so hard to squelch even the thought that something other than evolution is responsible for life?

I believe it's because pure evolution promotes a completely godless philosophy or view of the earth and humanity. Satan has worked very hard and has been quite successful at keeping God out of our classrooms and other institutions. When humanists teach evolution as a fact and don't allow any other viewpoints on the subject of creation, they close the door for any possible seeds to be planted in people's minds—and hearts—that God exists.

Ironically, at the Scopes "Monkey Trial" in 1925, where evolutionists were granted the right to present evolution as a theory in American classrooms, it was said to be a travesty of justice that only one theory of life origin—which at that time was creationism—should be taught. Yet, that is exactly what is happening today, except the single theory now being taught is evolution.

Dr. Carl Baugh, the founder of the Creation Evidence Museum in Glen Rose, Texas, is an ex-atheist who became a Christian and creationist. He also believes that evolution is a spiritual battle-ground. "It's not only a battle for the minds of men; it's a battle for their souls."[28] Another atheist-turned-creationist, Dr. Grady McMurtry, who developed Creation Worldview Ministries, adds: "Without the doctrine of creation, there is no Christianity.... If you start with Genesis...then take a look at John chapter 1 and Revelation 14:6 and 7, it is creation which is the foundation of Christianity. Without [creation] there is no Christianity."[29]

In the beginning was the Word, and the Word was with God, and the Word was God. The same was in the beginning with God. All things were made by him; and without him was not any thing made that was made. In him was life; and the life was the light of men. And the light shineth in darkness; and the darkness comprehended it not.

John 1:1–5

And I saw another angel fly in the midst of heaven, having the everlasting gospel to preach unto them that dwell on the earth, and to every nation, and kindred, and tongue, and people, saying with a loud voice, Fear God, and give glory to him; for

[28] Dr. Carl Baugh, interview with Andrew Wommack, March 6, 2012, Creation Evidence Museum, Glen Rose, TX.
[29] Dr. Grady McMurtry, interview with Andrew Wommack, June 8, 2012, Woodland Park, CO.

the hour of his judgment is come: and worship him that made heaven, and earth, and the sea, and the fountains of waters.

Revelation 14:6–7

Being totally pro-evolution allows people to deaden their heart to the voice of creation. According to Psalm 19, creation is shouting out to us:

The heavens declare the glory of God; and the firmament sheweth his handywork. Day unto day uttereth speech, and night unto night sheweth knowledge.

There is no speech nor language, where their voice is not heard. Their line is gone out through all the earth, and their words to the end of the world.

Psalm 19:1–4

Every day, people everywhere, even in the farthest reaches of this planet, are within shouting distance for creation to let them know there's a Creator. But people want to believe in evolution because it eliminates that voice, therefore eliminating account-ability to a Creator. If we evolved from slime and are nothing but evolved animals, then we can live like animals. And when we die, it's over—period. We didn't come from anywhere and aren't going anywhere, so we can do whatever we want. People who think this way conclude they can do whatever they want as long as they don't get caught or suffer any consequences. They simply establish their own morality.

However, the Bible is filled with details of God holding people accountable for their actions. God often pronounced judgment and punishment because people went against His commands. We, as His creation, are responsible to Him. One example is when the Lord became upset at mankind and wiped out everyone except Noah and his family (Genesis 6).

So many places in Scripture prove that we didn't evolve and that God is not some disinterested person out "there" who just wound the earth up like a clock and let it run. He created everything we see. He created us. His fingerprints are everywhere, and all of creation screams that at us. I believe evolution is being so heavily pushed down people's throats because it's an attempt to drown out that voice of creation.

Dr. McMurtry believes, "According to evolutionists, we're only thinking animals. ...Evolution is absolutely a religion. It is not science. It's a religion of convenience, meaning, if it's not convenient, it doesn't fit my religion.... [Evolutionists] want to believe it because it's the only way in which they can intellectually justify that they can lead a sinless life without Jesus Christ....this is what justifies the homosexual lifestyle, abortion, euthanasia, racism, pornography, all of our social ills....These social issues are merely the branches. The tree trunk is secular humanism, and evolution is the tap root."[30]

It's dangerous for anyone to fall into the evolution trap because it keeps that person from God. But it's especially hard

---

[30] Ibid.

to understand a Christian falling for it. The fundamental problem with evolution, like any other secular philosophy, is that it violates the Word of God. If, as a Christian, you embrace evolution and believe it to be true, you are ultimately going to disbelieve God's Word. Evolution is not compatible with the Bible.

I know there are Christians reading this who believe in evolution because that's what you've been taught. You've drunk the Kool-Aid without ever questioning its content. It's been reinforced millions and millions of times, and it seems like all of the movers and the shakers of our world believe it, so you should too. But at the same time, you'll claim that you believe the Bible. You can't have it both ways. If you truly believe in evolution, then you're going to have to believe that the Word of God is not accurate. By believing in evolution, you lose confidence in the authority that God's Word holds, which in turn will destroy your faith.

There is not one particular theory of evolution; there are many different theories. This is another problem with the whole evolution argument, because even among evolutionists, they can't agree on which theory is correct. In general, there are two categories of theories: anti-theistic theories, which basically state that our universe is here by a random accident and not because an intelligent being created it; and theistic theories, which hold that God did create the universe, but evolution was still part of the equation. Yet another theory is intelligent design, which claims that there was some sort of being—not necessarily God—who created life.

Biblical creationism, which views creation as a literal six-day event, and anti-theistic evolution, are polar opposites of one another, while all these other theories create an evolution spectrum in between. Sadly, many Christians believe in one of the many non-biblical theories of evolution, holding creationism views that have subtly evolved away from the truth of Scripture.

One of Satan's greatest tactics is to mix just enough truth with lies that we fall for the lies and into deception. Over time, he has masterfully created hybrids—theistic evolutionary theories—between evolution and creationism to the point where many Christians no longer have an untainted biblical view of how and when God formed the earth.

An example of theistic evolution is the thought that God was responsible for the Big Bang, but that living beings evolved from that point. Another is that God did form each creature, including humans, as individual and unique entities, but He did so millions of years ago. One version of this theory is called the gap theory, which states that there are actually millions of years of time between Genesis 1:1 ("In the beginning God created the heaven and the earth") and Genesis 1:2 ("And the earth was without form, and void; and darkness was upon the face of the deep. And the Spirit of God moved upon the face of the waters").

I've got friends who love God and love His Word who have bought into this theory, but I can't subscribe to it. They believe that prior to Genesis 1:2 there were hundreds of millions of years that existed, and during this time all of the dinosaurs were alive and there was an entire pre-Adamic civilization. They believe that what Genesis is explaining is actually a re-creation, not an original creation, of the earth.

Some Christians believe that there was a civilization in which Lucifer, who we now call Satan, populated this earth and ruled over it. Lucifer then rebelled against God, and God destroyed the demonic civilization, causing the earth to become vain and void (see Genesis 1:2). They believe that when God told Adam and Eve to replenish the earth (Genesis 1:28), the word *replenish* indicates that the earth was once vibrant; it was once full of life, but then it was destroyed. To those who believe this, Genesis 1:28 is describing the re-creation where Adam and Eve had to replenish—or refill—the earth.

I admit that the word *replenish* can mean to fill again, but this word is used a number of times in Scripture, and it's not talking about filling again; it simply means "to fill." In fact, all of the main translations of the Bible interpret this verse as "Be fruitful and fill the earth." It doesn't imply any of the meaning of refilling as some think.

Too many people, including Christians, won't stand and speak against evolution because they've been told that it's an established fact. They're taught that evolution has been proven over and over, so often, people are afraid to stand up and say anything about it. I was shocked to read an article that showed only a slight majority of pastors believe in biblical creationism. But even among those who do believe it, the vast majority won't teach it because they fear how their people will respond.

But there are currently thousands upon thousands of scientists who don't buy into the lie of evolution. Some believe in intelligent design and others believe in biblical creationism. Even though we're all told that evolution is an established fact, they understand that it's not. It's merely a theory—and one with many holes.

I believe in biblical creationism because I believe the Bible. The Word of God is sufficient for me to settle the issue of evolution versus creationism. But I realize that there are many Christians, even some of you reading this book, who may honor God's Word to a degree, but you also—maybe even more so—honor the natural and secular views you've been taught through our educational system. For this reason, I also want to approach this topic from a place of logic and science, using experts in the field who've discovered evidence supporting biblical creationism, to showcase the multitude of problems surrounding the theory of evolution.

First, let me share some things from Scripture. I encourage you to read through Genesis 1 on your own. Do so with an open mind and an open heart, and allow the Holy Spirit to speak to you through the scriptures. You'll see in Genesis that the Bible clearly states how God created the heavens and the earth:

In the beginning God created the heaven and the earth. And the earth was without form, and void; and darkness was upon the face of the deep. And the Spirit of God moved upon the face of the waters. And God said, Let there be light: and there was

light... And God said, Let there be lights in the firmament
of the heaven to divide the day from the night; and let them
be for signs, and for seasons, and for days, and years: And let
them be for lights in the firmament of the heaven to give light
upon the earth: and it was so. And God made two great lights;
the greater light to rule the day, and the lesser light to rule the
night: he made the stars also.

Genesis 1:1–3, 14–16

In verse 3, God spoke light into existence. He spoke light into existence before He created the sun, moon, or stars. That's what the Bible says. In other words, He spoke light into existence before there was a place for light to come from (v. 16). This by itself, totally disproves the Big Bang theory. These verses refute that theory because there was light before there was the sun, moon, and stars. The earth existed before the sun existed. There wasn't a bunch of matter that was just flung out in space. God created the earth, then on the third day He made the sun, moon, and stars and placed them in the heavens to give light to the earth. If you believe the Bible's account of creation, there isn't room to believe evolution.

Even if you believe there was a God who made the process of evolution happen, things didn't happen in the sequence that evolutionists say they did. The earth was created first. It was totally covered by water, and God spoke light into existence. It wasn't until the third day when He created the sun, moon, and stars. This is hard to understand because if you need light, you flip a light switch or grab a flashlight. The light comes from that source. But Romans 4:17 tells us that God "calleth those things which be not as though they were."

God simply speaks things into existence. God spoke light into existence before He created a source for light. I know that's hard for our brains to wrap around and understand, but it doesn't disprove it. Just because we can't understand how God did something and because it's not the way we would've done it doesn't mean it isn't true.

Dr. Baugh once reported on a graduate project conducted at UCLA where the students used a flask of water and a boom box from which they could control the sound frequencies. They discovered that when they generated certain frequencies, a small bubble appeared in the center of a flask of water. They later found by experimentation that the bubble heated to a hundred thousand degrees, yet was self-insulating. As it heated, out the other side of the bubble, a full spectrum of light was emitted.

Commenting on these results, Dr. Baugh said, "What happened in this experiment totally verifies Scripture. God said in the presence of that sphere of water that He had just created, 'Let there be light,' and there was light… from sound."[31]

We know that physicists have learned that at the base of every physical entity are cells made of atoms, which in turn are made of subatomic particles. All of these subatomic particles are vibrating.

---

[31] Dr. Carl Baugh, interview with Andrew Wommack, March 6, 2012, Creation Evidence Museum, Glen Rose, TX.

They have discovered that at the base of that vibration is sound. This confirms exactly what the Bible says! Everything we see was created by words, is maintained by words, and responds to words.

One big problem I've always had with the pro-evolution argument is that it's based on the assumption that the universe goes from disorder to order and from simple to complex. But this is the exact opposite of what really happens in nature, as stated in the Second Law of Thermodynamics. In fact, the popular evolutionist and anti-creationist Isaac Asimov admitted: "The Second Law of Thermodynamics states that the amount of available work you can get out of the energy of the universe is constantly decreasing. ...This is true for everything in general, the universe all over.[32] ...Another way of stating the second law then is, 'The universe is constantly getting more disorderly!' Viewed that way we can see the second law all about us. ...everything deteriorates, collapses, breaks down, wears out, all by itself—and that is what the second law is all about."[33]

This is totally contrary to the theory of evolution. In evolution, everything goes from very simple to incredibly complex and sophisticated. This is not observable anywhere in nature.

Dr. Baugh adds, "Basic life forms are more complicated than evolution can ever hope to address. Evolutionists like to say that

---

[32] Isaac Asimov, "The Origin of the Universe" *ORIGINS: How the World Came to Be, DVD,* Eden Communications, 1983.
[33] Isaac Asimov, "In the Game of Energy and Thermodynamics You Can't Even Break Even," *Smithsonian Institution Journal* (June 1970), 6.

changes take place over time. What they don't say is that that change has boundaries. So they slip in the concept that a tadpole can ultimately become a monkey that can ultimately become a PhD. But that change has limitations, and that change never leads to a higher order. It never increases the complexity. It might isolate the gene pool to get a superior product temporarily, but you have not increased the complexity. You have only limited the viability....Change over time is limited, and the final product is always downhill."[34]

To put this concept in simple terms, you can breed dogs, horses, and cows and get changes within that species, but at the end of the day, they are still dogs, horses, and cows. Mankind, with all its intelligence, can't breed a dog to become a cow or a monkey or a man. Change is limited to variations within that specific species. If it can't be done on purpose with intelligent thought and design, then it certainly can't happen accidentally.

Scripture backs this up. The Lord said in Genesis 1:11 that the grass and herbs were to bring forth "after their kind." In Genesis 1:21, all the sea creatures and fowl of the air "brought forth after their kind." Genesis 1:24-25 states:

And God said, Let the earth bring forth the living creature after his kind, cattle, and creeping thing, and beast of the earth after his kind: and it was so. And God made the beast of the earth after his kind, and cattle after their kind, and every thing that creepeth upon the earth after his kind: and God saw that it was good.

---

[34] Dr. Carl Baugh, interview with Andrew Wommack, March 6, 2012, Creation Evidence Museum, Glen Rose, TX.

Scripture clearly teaches that each species reproduces after its own kind. According to the command of God, it's impossible for one species to evolve into another species. For those who believe in the authority of the Bible, that kills evolution. But sadly, many Christians don't let the Bible get in the way of what they believe.

I believe in de-evolution. I can see in nature, and I see in the Bible, where humanity and other life forms have gone from complex to simple and from order to disorder. For instance, I believe that Adam was incredibly smart. It is said that people today only use about 10 percent of their brain. I have no way of knowing how they came to that conclusion. I think these people may use a lot less than 10 percent! But I do believe that Adam was hitting on all cylinders. God created man to be incredibly smart.

Adam was able to name every animal on earth. Their names are so descriptive of their function and how they live; this shows incredible intelligence on Adam's part. I believe that Adam and Eve were super smart, and I believe that we've all evolved downward from there. Evolution says that people came from apes, and they started out as cavemen who had no sophistication. Yet if you look at the oldest skeletons we have of mankind, they show incredible sophistication.

I also believe that we used to have a much deeper revelation of God. Adam and Eve walked with God in perfection, and Adam lived to be 930 years old. Adam had an intimate relationship with God and saw the creation in its perfection. Then he began to see the animals start to cannibalize each other, where in the beginning they were all herbivorous. Enoch also walked with God and had such a close relationship with Him that he was literally caught up into the heavens (see Genesis 5:24). He never died. He lived for over 300 years. The revelation of God that Adam and Enoch passed on impacted people!

People started out knowing God. Cain, when he killed Abel, spoke directly to God (see Genesis 4:9–16). They were having an audible, face-to-face confrontation. People started out knowing that there was a God, but we have devolved. When people say there is no God, that's reverse evolution. It's foolish! It goes against their intuitive knowledge (Romans 1:18-20).

> *The fool hath said in his heart, There is no God. They are corrupt, they have done abominable works, there is none that doeth good. The Lord looked down from heaven upon the children of men, to see if there were any that did understand, and seek God. They are all gone aside, they are all together become filthy: there is none that doeth good, no, not one.*

> *Psalm 14:1–3*

According to this scripture, which is repeated in Psalm 53, only a fool would say there is no God. Only a fool could look at creation and not figure out that this incredible complexity could not possibly evolve.

Take one of the simplest things in nature—a single blade of grass. If you pooled all the intellectual and financial resources of mankind, we could not produce a single, living, blade of grass. We could produce something that looks like grass; it might have the same texture and chemical makeup, but it couldn't reproduce itself. It wouldn't be alive.

If man, with all his intelligence can't do that which is least, then how can anyone possibly believe that the incredible complexity of nature could happen randomly? That defies logic. The chances of evolution happening randomly are impossible.

The chances of a 747 jet being perfectly assembled and able to fly as the result of a bomb going off at the Boeing Aircraft factory are infinitely more probable than the chances of evolution. The chances of an explosion in a print shop creating perfectly printed, bound, and stacked Bibles are infinitely more probable than the chances of evolution.

If spacecraft discovered a house on Mars, I guarantee that people would see this as proof that there was once life on that planet. They wouldn't think this house just evolved. Only an intelligent creature could create something like that. Yet, so-called "intellectuals" look at the complexity of nature and think it just evolved. That's foolish.

Perhaps you're reading this and acknowledging that you don't fully believe in evolution to the point where you think the earth is here by accident, but you have bought into some of the other theistic theories of creation. In this case, you still have mixed truth with lies and have adopted a secular worldview of how our earth was made. This is damaging to your faith. If you can't accept the Word at face value but instead mix other ingredients with it, your faith will become compromised. Satan can then easily get you to doubt the integrity of the rest of God's Word. This puts everything you believe about the Bible at risk.

Biblical creationism, which follows the whole truth of Scripture, is also called the young earth theory by scientists. It holds that the earth and every living creature was made by a Creator in a period of six days, just as stated in Genesis 1. Based on these verses, creation covered a span of six days—literal days, because each had a morning and an evening and because this is the same type of day referred to in Exodus 20:8–11, where the Sabbath is discussed. Jesus confirmed that humans were created at the same time as the earth (without millions of years separating them) when He said, "From the beginning of the creation God made them male and female" (Mark 10:6). Any other view of creation is, in some form, a compromise of what Scripture teaches.

Dr. Grady McMurtry wholeheartedly believes in a young earth theory. But this was not always the case. Dr. McMurtry grew up learning evolution in the public schools of Berkeley, California. He also spent time in the paleontology labs of University of California Berkeley, learning about dinosaur fossils and evolutionary theory as a child. He learned so much that when he was only eight years old, teachers started "borrowing" him from one classroom to another to teach other kids! He ultimately went on to earn a MS from State University of New York in evolutionary theory, which he later taught.

But when McMurtry was 27, the Holy Spirit guided him through Scripture and proved to him that Jesus was who He said

He was, and he became a Christian. He immediately recognized that he couldn't reconcile what he was reading in the Bible about creation with his evolution background. **After sixteen months of study and research, he came to the conclusion that there is not one law of science or one natural process that sufficiently supports evolution, whereas every natural law, every natural process, and all of the earth's physical evidence supports creation.**

Now, after decades of continued research, McMurtry travels the world educating people on the case for a young earth. "Whether you look in the earth, on the earth, or outside of the earth in space, there is plenty of evidence to show the earth is young," he argues.[35] In fact, McMurtry states that there are over 270 geochronometers, or earth time clocks, that demonstrate a recent creation of the universe.

For example, minerals and gemstones found inside the earth are said by evolutionists to take millions of years to form. But Dr. McMurtry has found evidence of gold being formed in fewer than five hours, and states that in 2006 it was discovered how to produce flawless diamonds in fewer than twelve hours.[36] McMurtry also points to stalagmites, which supposedly take millions of years to grow, having formed on Mayan pottery made in AD 700, as evidence of a young earth.[37]

---

[35] Dr. Grady McMurtry, *Why I Believe in a Young Creation*, DVD, Creation Worldview Ministries, 2009.
[36] Ibid.
[37] Ibid.

My own study found that granite contains a radioactive particle called polonium 214, having a half-life of .000164 seconds. That means this radioactive particle dissipates in less than one-one thousandth of a second. If it took more than one-one thousandth of a second for granite to form, polonium 214 wouldn't be trapped in the rock.

Dr. McMurtry also views the decay of the earth's magnetic field as further evidence of a young earth. Earth's decay has been measurable since the early 1800s. The earth decays in the same way that radioactive material does, meaning it has a half-life. The half-life of the earth's magnetic field is 1400 years. So, every 1400 years, one half of the strength of the magnetic field decays. Going back in time 1400 years, the strength of this field would double. Our magnetic field bends the sun's radiation at the poles, and without it everything on earth would die. Ten thousand years ago, the strength of the field would have killed all life on earth; therefore living beings couldn't have been here millions of years ago, as old earth theorists claim.

Yet, the further we move ahead in time, the weaker the field becomes. Within 2000 years, our current magnetic field will be gone. As Dr. McMurtry put it, "We live in a very narrow band of time. This is why we know that Jesus is coming back soon, because when He comes there will still be people on earth. That means the field has to still be strong enough to shield the earth from the sun's radiation. God never intended the earth to last a long time once it became flawed due to human sin."[38]

---

[38] Ibid.

Chapter 10 Illustrations

The World Ocean Floor Map.

Figure 1–From page 202

Pangaea Globe.

Figure 2–From page 203

Stretch Marks in the Indian Ocean.

Figure 3–From page 203

The Layers in the Rocky Mountains.

Figure 4–From page 205

Redwall Limestone & Cambrian Muav layers interlaced
in the Grand Canyon.

Figure 5–From page 205

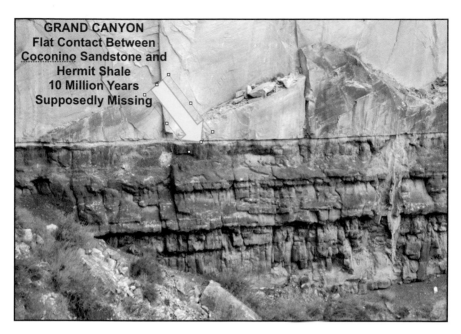

GRAND CANYON
Flat Contact Between
Coconino Sandstone and
Hermit Shale
10 Million Years
Supposedly Missing

Missing layers (according to evolutionary thinking).

Figure 6–From page 205

Rapid layer development at Mt. St. Helens. The ash formed
a 75 foot cliff with 3 separate "zones" each 25 feet deep.

Figure 7–From page 206

Mt. St. Helens proves how fast a canyon can be cut.

Figure 8–From page 207

Mississippi River Delta from space- Mud accumulations at the mouth of the world's rivers prove the Earth to be about 6000 years old.

Figure 9–From page 207

Dinosaur print overlapping a human foot print.

Figure 10–From page 210

Human footprints from the Lueders Formation in the Permian Basin
which evolutionists falsely estimate to be 230 million years old.

Figure 12–From page 210

A human sandal print with stitching around the sides, which proves a developed man. Found in the Permian Basin (where evolutionists believe these rock layers would have formed millions of years before man even existed).

Figure 13–See page 212

A man-made hammer found in early Cretaceous rock, once again showing that humans were alive at the same time these rock layers were formed.

Figure 14–From page 213

Chapter 13 Images
Abortion

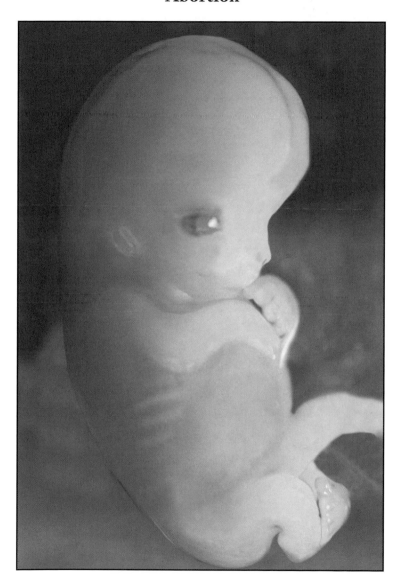

Week 5: The eyes, legs and hands begin to develop.

Figure 15–From page 256

Image Source: http://www.nrlc.org/abortion/facts/fetaldevelopment.html

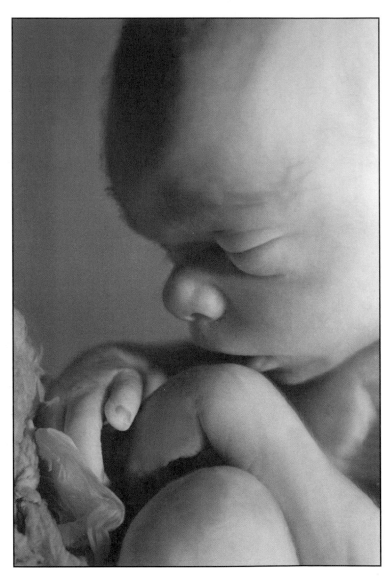

Week 17: The baby can have dream (REM) sleep.

Figure 16–From page 257

What absolutely convinces Dr. McMurtry of a young earth is the evidence he's seen in the world's rock formations, along with sediment that has formed in the mouths of rivers across the globe. He thoroughly believes these things point to a global event of catastrophic proportions that very quickly changed the face of the earth—an event that perfectly harmonizes with the Flood in the Bible. The following is taken from an interview I conducted with Dr. McMurtry where he explains his findings.[39]

****

Let's start with Day 3 of creation to show how Noah's Flood is related to the way God made the earth. On Day 3, God caused the dry land to rise out of the water, and He gathered the seas, which are shallow—only up to a mile deep. He gathered the water into one place, and dry land appeared. There are separations of waters above and below, and in this firmament God made what we call the earth's crust, but it's more like an eggshell. Ten miles underneath is a layer of water one mile deep, which we found evidence of in 1909. We now know that there are large pockets of water down there that never came up the first time and that there is at least five to six times more water in the crust than on the crust. At ten miles of depth, the earth warms at 90 degrees per mile initially, so that water is 900 degrees Fahrenheit.

At this temperature, the water is liquid steam, the same thing that causes volcanic eruptions. God put it down there, knowing He'd need it 1,656 years later. Genesis 7:11 says that the fountains

---

[39] Dr. Grady McMurtry, interview with Andrew Wommack, June 8, 2012, Woodland Park, CO.

of the great deep, or the springs of waters, burst forth or broke open. The actual Hebrew word used is *cleave*. *Cleave* means "to come into a knife edge." The waters knifed through from below to start the Flood. The World Ocean Floor Map (Fig. 1) shows the

See the World Ocean Floor Map (Fig.1) on page 193.

exact places where the waters knifed through. It also shows how the continents were separated by this water bursting forth. They floated rapidly because they're on a layer of water. Although the continents are in one piece to start with, when they were knifed through, they broke into smaller pieces.

During earthquakes, land cracks open, presenting an opportunity for hot rock and hot water to come up from below. Initially the water is trapped, but when the earth breaks open, the waters knife through the crack. Caesarea Philippi is where the land crack of the Flood began. It started very, very tight, which is what will happen with tremendous pressure at one point. From there, the crack went down to what is now the Jordan River and then to the Red Sea. It continued underneath the ocean into the Indian Ocean, going around the world 40,000 miles, breaking all three continents from the others. This one continuous crack shows it was the result of one specific occurrence and not separate events.

The significance of the crack starting at Caesarea Philippi is beyond belief. This is where Jesus led His disciples and asked them, "Who do men say the Son of Man is?" Then He asked one of the two most important questions in the entire New Testament: "Who do *you* say that I am?" He asks that at the very spot where the crack starts and breaks off three continents. It's the very place where the Jordan River starts as clear living water coming out of a rock. This is not a coincidence. Jesus knew exactly where He was. He was there before the crack was!

Evolutionists talk about Pangaea, or how all the continents used to fit together, which is a biblical concept. You can see on the Pangaea Globe (Fig. 2)—although you can tell better on a round

See the Pangaea Globe (Fig.2) on page 193.

globe—how the continental shelf of Greenland perfectly fits the continental shelf of Norway. It's like two pieces of a jigsaw puzzle. Then there's a crack going up the middle where the eruption of hot rock and hot water took place when the waters cleaved from below. You can also see how the western continental shelf of New Zealand perfectly fits the eastern continental shelf of Australia.

And, you can see stretch marks in the Indian Ocean (Fig. 3),

See the Indian Ocean stretch marks (Fig.3) on page 193.

which only happen when something occurs quickly, like a nine-month pregnancy. If evolution was true and it took hundreds of millions of years, you wouldn't see the stretch marks because there would be deep layers of mud due to years and years of rain washing sediment off the continents. But we do see stretch marks, and we have what are called abyssal plains, or flat sand bottoms, right up against the side of the continents. This proves that mud never came into the Atlantic in the first place, meaning this all formed in a short period of time.

Now, the mountains before the Flood were up to 5,000 feet high but were capable of being covered with one mile of water. The water eroded those mountains that existed from creation to the Flood and created the wet mud layers—the sedimentary rock layers—that were re-deposited. Seventy-five to eighty percent of the earth's land surface is covered with dried-out mud layers, or sedimentary rock, containing trillions of dead plants and animals that all drowned. That should be proof enough of a worldwide flood, not a slow and gradual accumulation.

After the Flood ended, the layers eroded, and other layers were lifted and folded by tectonic forces, the moving of continents and so forth. This process occurs while the layers are still wet, and then only after they have been folded do they dry into hard rock. We see these folded layers all over the world, showing how everything was deposited very quickly and proving a rapid formation. We also know that fossilization is rapid, and to form a fossil something has to be buried rapidly, otherwise it would decay. Yet we have fossils all through these mud layers.

Experiments in Colorado State University's sedimentation laboratory prove that all layers form at the same time and merely extend in the direction of water flow. With moving water, the bottom and top layers form at the same time but extend as the water flows in that direction. The layer in the bottom is the same age as the layer on the top, which totally disproves evolution.

The layers in the Rocky Mountains (Fig. 4) are easy to see. If evolution was true, these layers should be flat because water seeks

See the layers in the Rocky Mountains (Fig.4) on page 194.

its own level and lays down flat. But instead of flat layers, there are undulations or wavelike layers, again showing a rapid formation. More evidence is the erosion material at the bottom. If those mountains are 300 million years old, there's not nearly enough erosion material. The erosion material present only supports a formation time of a few thousand years.

In the Grand Canyon (Fig. 5) there are Redwall Limestone and Cambrian Muav layers interlaced. There's one then another then

See the interlaced layers (Fig.5) on page 194.

another going back and forth, showing that the canyon was not clean cut like evolutionists say it should be if the layers have different ages. Rather, it reflects water currents depositing layer after layer of material as they moved back and forth. We even have layers that are missing, according to evolutionary thinking (Fig. 6). Sometimes there are smooth flat lines, but there are ten million years missing.

See the missing layers (Fig.6) on page 195.

Also, if, as evolutionists claim, the layers were deposited at different times, there had to be some period during which each layer was exposed before the next layer was deposited. But there are no soil horizons, or places where rock eroded into soil, in between the layers. There also are no V-shape erosion marks, which occur when the layers are exposed to rain. Those erosion marks should be filled in by the next layer of mud, but evidence of that is not there. And there are no animal holes or root holes. The lack of these things shows that all these layers were deposited at one time in a really big flood, and they were not exposed one after another after another.

We can also look at the eruption of Mount St. Helens in 1980 to show how the Grand Canyon was formed quickly. During the initial nine hours of eruption on May 18, twenty-five feet of ash was laid down in one layer. The second layer is actually comprised of several layers that formed during a second eruption over a period of five hours. Again, these layers are about twenty-five feet deep. The top layer, also about twenty-five feet, formed in fewer than twenty-four hours. There were three distinct events during the time of the eruptions from 1980 to 1982. But all three layers—a total of seventy-five feet—came into existence in fewer than three days. This shows that geological features form quite rapidly.

We have eye-witness documentation and photographic evidence to prove the time frame in which these layers developed (Fig. 7). The ash formed a seventy-five-foot cliff with three separate

See how the layers developed (Fig.7) on page 195.

"zones," each twenty-five feet deep. Evolutionists would believe that this material came into existence at the rate of one inch every thousand to ten thousand years by the erosion of prior rock material. Therefore, to an evolutionist, this cliff would represent one million years worth of history. In reality, it represents three days.

Evolutionists would also want you to believe that all the layers of the Grand Canyon came about slowly and gradually over millions of years and that the Colorado River cut the canyon just as slowly and gradually. The first problem with that is a river that small could not cut such a big canyon. Second, we have another example from Mount St. Helens to prove how fast a canyon can be cut (Fig. 8). This 125-foot-deep canyon was cut in one day by

See how fast a canyon can be cut (Fig.8) on page 196.

mudflow. This just shows that massive amounts of water or mud moving very quickly all at once can do a tremendous amount of work. There's no reason why an event such as Noah's Flood could not have carved the Grand Canyon in less than a year.

We can also look at mud accumulation at the mouths of the world's rivers to prove the earth has only been around for about 6000 years. One example is the Mississippi River (Fig. 9). The

Mud accumulations prove Earth's age (Fig.9) on page 196.

Gulf of Mexico is a big empty hole in the ground with a flat sand surface on the bottom, but there is only 4500 years worth of mud at the mouth of the Mississippi. If the Mississippi were millions of years old, the entire Gulf of Mexico would be filled in. This is one of the simplest and easiest ways to see that the earth is young. And every major river in the world is the same way. The Amazon, the Colorado River that goes all the way into the Baja, the Indus Ganges, and so forth - all of them only have 4,500 years worth of mud at their mouths, showing that the earth has only been eroding since the time of Noah's Flood.

****

It's obvious that Dr. McMurtry has compiled quite a bit of research that goes a long way toward validating biblical creationism while also demonstrating many of the problems with the pro-evolution argument. But whenever evolution versus creationism is discussed, people always want to know about the fossils, especially the dinosaurs. In addition visiting with Dr. McMurtry, I've also spent considerable time with Dr. Carl Baugh, who has personally excavated many, many fossils during his time in paleontology.

Like Dr. McMurtry, Dr. Baugh is an ex-atheist who used to teach evolution. He has doctorate degrees in education, theology, and biblical archaeology. His most recent work has been in the paleontology field where he has discovered and directed the excavation of sixteen different dinosaurs. The following information is what Dr. Baugh discussed with me as he presented his case for a young earth.[40]

****

Dr. Ernst Mayr, who's considered to be the world's leading evolutionary biologist, said if there's proof that man and dinosaur lived at the same time, evolution is destroyed. Well, I found that proof in 1982 when my excavation team unearthed a dinosaur footprint and a human footprint only seventeen inches apart. But,

---

[40] Dr. Carl Baugh, interview with Andrew Wommack, March 6, 2012, Creation Evidence Museum, Glen Rose, TX.

not surprisingly, none of the scientists or media would even look at the findings because they assumed it was a hoax.

We discovered a very large acrocanthosaurus along the banks of the Paluxy River in Texas, and the other dinosaurs we found in northwestern Colorado. But the one along the Paluxy completely shattered my entire paradigm, because coming into that excavation I was an old-age creationist. I had heard but didn't believe that there were human footprints right along with dinosaur footprints near the Paluxy River. In 1982, I came out to direct the excavation. I assimilated a team, and we excavated one dinosaur footprint. Then, over the course of four days, we excavated another eighteen footprints.

I still didn't believe we'd find human footprints because I adhered to the view of evolution in which the last dinosaur died out sixty-four million years ago, and the first human didn't appear, even in primitive form, until two and a half million years ago. I was what you could call a progressive creationist. But then, one day as we were peeling back the layers of rock, I discovered a human footprint only seventeen and a half inches from a dinosaur footprint. It completely blew my mind. We continued excavating and discovered a total of four of these human prints.

In this trail of dinosaur and human footprints, the dinosaur stepped on two of the human footprints and pushed its print back into the heel of the human print, compressing it. You can see the heel, the toes, the compression. The dinosaur actually pushed the mud into the human print.

And then it stepped on another one and cut it off (Fig. 10).

See the fossil print (Fig.10) on page 197.

[Author's note: I personally saw these fossils at the Creation Evidence Museum in Glen Rose, Texas, when I was interviewing Dr. Baugh. They are very clearly human and dinosaur prints side by side and on top of each other. It's somewhat hard to determine from these photos, but I can personally verify that they are clearly visible.]

On another occasion, we found a series of human footprints from the Lueders Formation in the Permian Basin in West Texas. According to evolution, the hard sandstone of the Permian Basin is about 230 million years old, so there shouldn't be any human prints in it. We took those prints to two separate laboratories and ran spiral CAT scan analyses on them, which reads through the rock to determine if the print is genuine. Every one of these footprints had compression density under it and to its side, mimicking the way a real foot would move (Fig. 12).

See the human footprint in Permian Basin (Fig.12) on page 197.

[Author's note: I'm aware that many people, even some creation scientists, have discounted these footprints because there was a man in Glen Rose, Texas, who carved dinosaur and human footprints together to make money during the Great Depression. Therefore, all evidence from Glen Rose is considered to be false. But as Dr. Baugh explained to me, these spiral CAT scans can detect compression density; they can determine if the imprint was carved or made by the weight of an actual foot. All of Dr. Baugh's samples have been proven to be actual prints made by humans and dinosaurs.]

Although the media who've come to view our discoveries always find a way to explain away what they're seeing with their own eyes, we've had many evolutionists come who leave as creationists. Recently a leading evolutionary scholar became a creationist, and one of my friends said to him, "I thought you were an evolutionist and taught evolution."

He said, "I was, and I did."

"What changed you?" my friend asked.

"Well," he said, "I kept watching and reading about the evidence that Carl Baugh in Glen Rose, Texas, presented, and I couldn't ignore it."

Even Dr. Antony Flew, one of the world's leading atheists, a few years ago turned his back on evolution after visiting our friends at The Institute for Creation Research. Dr. Flew admitted in writing that he has taught atheism and was one of the world's leading atheists, but The Institute for Creation Research exposed enough information that he can no longer deny that living systems are so complex, they require a designer. These examples prove that when people have an open mind, the evidence will speak for itself.

Aside from discovering dinosaur and human prints in the Permian Basin, we've found man-made artifacts saturated throughout this system of rock layers. According to evolutionists, these rock layers would have been here millions of years before man even existed. One artifact we found was a human sandal print with stitching around its sides. The stitching proves this was from a developed man. This sandal even has wear on the heel from the transference of weight when we walk (Fig. 13).

See human sandal print in Permian Basin (Fig.13) on page 198.

What's even more interesting about this sandal is that it has a three-lobed sea bug pressed into the heel and another pressed into the toe. These sea bugs are supposedly around 550 million years old, and evolutionists put them at the bottom of the geological column because they're considered to be simple life forms. But some types of these bugs have compound eyes more sophisticated than any of today's most advanced cameras. And these bugs were found at the exact same time and place as a human sandal print!

Once I saw actual evidence that man and dinosaur lived contemporaneously, I searched for additional evidence. Over a period of time I've discovered a long series of artifacts, supposedly from the bottom of the geologic column, that are scattered throughout the geologic column. The director of a leading museum in Austria once called me to say that it's come to his attention that we have more out-of-place artifacts that destroy evolutionary theory than all other entities combined. And he's right!

Another discovery worth noting is a cup that was found encased in coal. It was found by Frank Kinard in 1928 as he was working in the Sulphur City Water Works, shoveling coal to use as electricity for the town. He had a huge chunk of coal that he couldn't fit into the furnace, so he took a sledgehammer to it, and it fell apart. A man-made cup fell out of it. Coal is said by evolutionists to take nearly 400 million years to form. Yet, we see evidence of coal and a man-made cup that are the same age (Fig. 14). Similarly, a man-made hammer was found buried in early Cretaceous rock, once again showing that humans were alive at the same time as these rock layers (Fig. 14).

See man-made tools in Cretaceous rock (Fig.14) on page 198.

I believe that all this evidence, along with other evidence that has been discovered over the years, absolutely disproves any form of evolution and decidedly points to a young earth, biblical creationism. But again, I don't have to have scientists help me reach this conclusion—I have the Word of God. You were created by God. If you truly believe that you somehow evolved, you will believe anything! If you can swallow that lie, I don't know what the limit would be on what you would believe.

Romans 1:18–20 tell us:

For the wrath of God is revealed from heaven against all ungodliness and unrighteousness of men, who hold the truth in unrighteousness; Because that which may be known of God is manifest in them; for God hath shewed it unto them. For the invisible things of him from the creation of the world are clearly seen, being understood by the things that are made, even his eternal power and Godhead; so that they are without excuse.

These are powerful passages of Scripture that basically say that the invisible things of God are revealed in us—not just to us, but in us. According to Psalm 19, creation is shouting out that there is a God! For anyone who pays attention this is obvious, but even beyond creation, we have an inner witness. God has put a homing device on the inside of every person. If we could "Be still and know that [He is] God" (Psalm 46:10), the Holy Spirit would reveal these things to us.

I'm sure there are people who disagree with everything I'm saying, and they just dismiss it. They won't even think about it. But why not? If what they believe is true, wouldn't it stand examination? If evolution is proven, as they believe, wouldn't all of the facts confirm it? Why would they be afraid to hear about facts that are contrary? The truth is that people refuse to acknowledge that which is contrary to their belief system. They won't confront it. I'm just being bold and telling you that you need to take time to evaluate the facts you've been presented with. Know that God has already revealed these truths to you on the inside.

Get still, get quiet, and open your heart and say, "God, show me if You created the heavens and the earth in six days and if evolution is wrong." Read the scriptures that I've presented here. Evaluate the information given by Dr. Carl Baugh and Dr. Grady McMurtry. If you give this viewpoint a chance, I believe that God will reveal Himself in you and to you. Those who are living an unrighteous lifestyle have a motivation for disbelieving in biblical creationism, and many have absolutely no conviction about any of this. The Bible says you can harden your heart (Hebrews 3:8).

You can have your conscience so seared that you can get to a place where you don't believe anything and you have no conviction from God (1 Timothy 4:2).

That doesn't change the fact that everyone, at one time, had an intuitive knowledge of God on the inside. I don't ever argue with an atheist. I go past all their arguments and just say, "You know the truth. You know that there's a God. If somebody were to put a gun to your head and tell you they're going to kill you, you'd call out to the God that you say you don't believe in." I go past their mind and arguments and straight to their heart.

There are some of you who've embraced evolution and have never challenged it. You haven't closely examined it. You've just accepted the lies you've been told. But I believe that deep down, you know that it isn't possible! If you will allow Him, the Holy Spirit will reveal to you that you were created and designed by God. You aren't a mistake. Whether your parents knew that you were coming or not, God created you.

For thou hast possessed my reins: thou hast covered me in my mother's womb. I will praise thee; for I am fearfully and wonderfully made: marvellous are thy works; and that my soul knoweth right well. My substance was not hid from thee, when I was made in secret, and curiously wrought in the lowest parts of the earth. Thine eyes did see my substance, yet being unperfect; and in thy book all my members were written, which in continuance were fashioned, when as yet there was none of them.

Psalm 139:13–16

Before I formed thee in the belly I knew thee; and before thou camest forth out of the womb I sanctified thee, and I ordained thee a prophet unto the nations.

Jeremiah 1:5

You didn't just randomly evolve. It's not up to you to pick and choose what you want to do. You were created, designed by God with a purpose. You are not an evolved animal; you are a created being. You are going to stand before God some day and give an account for what you did with your life. And you know this at a heart level. Whether your head agrees with it or not, your heart knows it. I encourage you to submit your heart to the Lord today and carefully and prayerfully examine what's just been presented to you.

For more information on Dr. Carl Baugh's ministry and museum, go to: www.creationevidence.org

To learn more about Dr. Grady McMurtry's ministry and research, visit his website at: www.creationworldview.org

You may also watch the interviews with Dr. Baugh and Dr. McMurtry by ordering my recent DVD series, "Christian Philosophy." To order, go to the Andrew Wommack Ministries website at www.awmi.net.

Chapter 11

A Godly Perspective on Homosexuality

G od is not a respecter of persons, and He doesn't grade us on a curve or sliding scale. All sin is evil, and Scripture says that if you have fallen short on one point, then you are guilty of the whole Law (James 2:10). So it would be wrong for a Christian to feel superior to homosexuals or to look at them and say, "Thank God, at least I'm not caught up in *that* kind of sin." Jesus warned against that attitude in His parable about the Pharisee and the publican:

Two men went up into the temple to pray; the one a Pharisee, and the other a publican. The Pharisee stood and prayed thus with himself, God, I thank thee, that I am not as other men are, extortioners, unjust, adulterers, or even as this publican. I fast twice in the week, I give tithes of all that I possess. And the publican, standing afar off, would not lift up so much as his eyes unto heaven, but smote upon his breast, saying, God be merciful to me a sinner. I tell you, this man went down to his house justified rather than the other: for every one that exalteth himself shall be abased; and he that humbleth himself shall be exalted.

Luke 18:10-14

Notice how Jesus said that the man merely living a holy life was not justified in the eyes of God. The sinner who repented was justified. We need to be careful in discussing moral issues that we don't fall into the trap of comparing ourselves among ourselves, and measuring our performance against the performance of others (2 Corinthians 10:12).

My purpose in discussing homosexuality is not to scold homosexuals or to prove what an ungodly act it is. The Bible is clear that homosexuality is wrong—just like adultery, lying, drunkenness, gluttony, and idolatry are sins—but in today's media, homosexuality is presented as an acceptable alternative lifestyle. I want to counter the misinformation floating around with a Christian philosophy and show that homosexuality is a destructive way of life—by any standard.

In 2009, President Obama held a lesbian, gay, bisexual, and transgender (known as LGBT) pride month reception at the White House at which he said, "There are unjust laws to overturn and unfair practices to stop. And though we've made progress, there are still fellow citizens, perhaps neighbors or even family members and loved ones, who still hold fast to worn arguments and old attitudes; who fail to see your families like their families; and who would deny you the rights that most Americans take for granted… we must recognize that real progress depends not only on the laws we change but, as I said before, on the hearts we open. For if we're honest with ourselves, we'll acknowledge that there are good and decent people in this country who don't yet fully embrace their gay brothers and sisters—not yet."[41]

The president's remarks accurately reflect the stance taken by the media and popular culture in America today. Homosexuality is seen as a way of life that is wrongfully discriminated against, and the LGBT community is pushing to gain legal protections. I agree that it is wrong to lash out against people practicing homosexuality, or to persecute them unfairly, but it isn't persecution to point out wrong behavior. Society has been manipulated into believing that calling homosexuality immoral is somehow inappropriate or "close-minded."

The gay rights movement got its start after the Stonewall riots in Greenwich Village, New York City, in 1969. The protests began after police raided a bar for being a gay establishment, and the gay patrons fought back. Soon a march was staged to Central Park to bring awareness, and the gay rights movement was born. In the early 1990s, the movement really began to make headway with the claim that homosexuality was genetic. Suddenly, in the minds of many, homosexuality transformed from being an immoral choice to being an unavoidable and irreversible condition of birth.

---

[41] Barack Obama, "Remarks by the President at LGBT Pride Month Reception" (speech, The White House, Washington, DC, June 29, 2009). http://www.whitehouse.gov/the_press_office/Remarks-by-the-President-at-LGBT-Pride-Month-Reception/

There are some Christians who are hesitant to accept that homosexuality is immoral when so many sources are claiming it is a condition of birth. They say, "How can God punish someone for something that they can't control? If God made them that way, then they have no choice." It's a good question. We know God wouldn't condemn anyone to eternal punishment for factors beyond their control, so the first thing we need to do is examine the claim that homosexual behavior is "genetic."

One of the studies that is used to promote the idea that homosexuality is genetic is a study of identical twins published by Bailey and Pillard in 1991. The investigation found that when one identical twin is gay, then the other twin is more likely to be gay also; meaning the other twin was more likely to be gay than another random person would be. The researchers noted that the findings were not proof that homosexuality is genetic, but the media ran with it anyway as sure evidence of the genetic link to being gay. They ignored other portions of the study, which showed that the rate of homosexuality among families with one gay twin was 200%-300% higher than average—this included among adopted siblings.[42] Adopted siblings obviously don't share a genetic link to the family with higher rates of homosexuality, so environmental factors were clearly the cause. In truth, this study makes a strong argument that homosexuality is *not* genetic.

---

[42] "Is Sexual Orientation genetic or is it a choice?" *Exodus Global Alliance*, Web, accessed July 1, 2011, http://www.exodusglobalalliance.org/causesc37.php

Still, some continue to claim that homosexual behavior has hormonal or other biological causes. The first attempts to attribute biological causes to homosexuality arose in the late 19th century and were built upon the scientific principles of the Enlightenment.[43] Here again, we see the influence that philosophy has upon how you interpret life. To a scientific naturalist, everything must be reduced to a physical cause, so they try to attribute a physical explanation for *all* behavior, including homosexuality. But naturalism is a flawed philosophy, not all behavior is reducible to a physical cause.

Other studies have pointed to differences in brain structure or function between heterosexuals and homosexuals, but it is well known that behavior and experience cause the brain to reorganize itself. This ability is referred to as neuroplasticity, and it occurs throughout life. In other words, repeated homosexual experiences or emotions can cause a change in brain structure, as opposed to the behavior being caused by brain structure. Additionally, no hormonal differences have been discovered between heterosexuals and homosexuals, which is a serious blow against the argument that homosexuality has a biological cause.

In 1975, the American Psychological Association buckled to political pressure and removed homosexuality from its list of mental disorders. Although the APA still does not view homosexuality as a

---

[43] Ranier Herrn PhD., "On the History of Biological Theories of Homosexuality," *Journal of Homosexuality*, Volume 28, Issue 1-2. Web, accessed July 1, 2011, http://www.tandfonline.com/doi/abs/10.1300/J082v28n01_03#preview

choice, they have been forced to admit that no conclusive evidence has been found to attribute homosexuality to biology. Their latest literature about homosexuality says, "Although much research has examined the possible genetic, hormonal, developmental, social, and cultural influences on sexual orientation, *no findings have emerged that permit scientists to conclude that sexual orientation is determined by any particular factor or factors*" (Emphasis mine).[44]

Despite how badly some want to attribute biological causes to homosexual behavior, no biological causes have ever been found. The media has overstated the implications of research and misinterpreted other data, but—as the American Psychological Association openly states—homosexuality cannot be defined as genetic or a condition of birth.

Many factors influence the shaping of our identity, but the bottom line is that homosexuality is a choice. Some people might be more tempted by homosexuality than others, but that doesn't make the choice of engaging in homosexual behavior any less immoral. In the same way, adultery is always wrong—no matter how great the temptation or how significant the environmental influences.

The apostle Paul wrote that no one engaging in a homosexual lifestyle will inherit the kingdom of God (1 Corinthians 6:9). Therefore, we know that homosexuality is a choice—not an innate condition. So it is important for Christians to speak the truth in

---

[44] American Psychological Association, "Sexual Orientation and Homosexuality: Answers to Your Questions for a Better Understanding," *APA.org*, 4. http://www.apa.org/topics/sexuality/orientation.aspx

love, rather than keep quiet and let people be deceived into believing that homosexuals aren't responsible for their choices. To keep quiet about the immorality of homosexuality would be contrary to God's command:

> *"Thou shalt not hate thy brother in thine heart: thou shalt in any wise rebuke thy neighbour, and not suffer sin upon him... but thou shalt love thy neighbour as thyself: I am the Lord."*
>
> *Leviticus 19:17–18*

I don't think I would need to spend much time convincing you that murder is immoral; we all intuitively know it is wrong. But the gay lobby has been so successful in promoting homosexuality as normal behavior that many Christians no longer view it as immoral.

The National Gay and Lesbian Task Force (NGLTF) has intentionally sought the endorsement of faith communities to increase the public perception that homosexuality is normal, and they have gained credibility by associating their agenda with established Christian denominations. Some denominations have even appointed homosexual men and women to leadership roles. This is in direct opposition to ministers who are being vocal about the immorality of homosexuality. The NGLTF says, "...it is [imperative] that the LGBT rights advocates work with and within communities of faith to reclaim from the right wing the true meaning of moral values,"[45] which shows they are inten-

---

[45] National Gay and Lesbian Task Force statement on faith, accessed July 5, 2011, http://www.thetaskforce.org/issues/faith

tionally infiltrating the church to undermine biblical values and promote the acceptance of homosexuality.

The gay lobby has been so successful at distorting the biblical perspective that we now have churches promoting the gay agenda—even though Scripture unambiguously denounces homosexuality. I understand having compassion toward people who are caught up in destructive behaviors and wanting to reach out to help them, but to endorse and promote homosexuality, you have to oppose the Word of God. This shocks me, but I have learned that there are many religious people who don't let the Word of God affect what they believe.

The story of Sodom very clearly reveals God's view of homosexuality. God sent two angels down to Sodom, and when Lot saw them, he invited them into his house to have a meal and spend the night. Scripture says that many of us have entertained angels unaware (Hebrews 13:2), which means they don't always appear with wings and halos above their heads. So the angels who visited Lot apparently looked like human beings, and every man in Sodom wanted to have sex with them.

> *But before they lay down, the men of the city, even the men of Sodom, compassed the house round, both old and young, all the people from every quarter: And they called unto Lot, and said unto him, Where are the men which came in to thee this night? bring them out unto us, that we may know them.*
>
> *Genesis 19:4-5*

A Godly Perspective on Homosexuality

The King James uses the verb "know" to refer to sexual relations, but some other translations render the passage more explicitly: "Where are the men who came to you tonight? Bring them out to us so that we can have sex with them" (NIV). Lot was repulsed by their demands and tried to stop the citizens of Sodom from accosting the angels. The angels struck everyone blind (Genesis 19:11) and led Lot and his family out of Sodom. Once they were safe, God rained brimstone and fire from heaven as judgment to destroy the entire city (Genesis 19:24). You simply cannot read the account of Sodom and think that God approves of homosexuality.

But God isn't striking homosexuals or adulterers dead anymore. Under the New Covenant, there is a cure for sin. Our born-again spirits make it possible for God to relate to us with mercy and grace. In the same way, we are called to deal with all sinners by grace, no matter what kind of sin they are caught up in—but that doesn't mean we ignore wrong behavior.

Christians can commit the sin of homosexuality in the same way that they can get addicted to pornography or commit adultery, but there is no such thing as a church that promotes adultery, pornography, or lying and stealing. Christians might do some of those immoral things, but we don't build churches around embracing and promoting destructive behaviors. So why are people forming church groups that promote homosexuality?

I have a few friends who have committed homosexual acts. They are still friends and I love them. I have helped them through those difficulties. God paid for the sin of homosexuality through

Jesus, so He is not going to send people to hell just for the sin of homosexuality. The sin of rejecting Jesus is what sends people to hell (John 16:9). The sin of homosexuality is forgiven because of Jesus' sacrifice, but God's Word is clear that homosexuality is wrong.

> *If a man also lie with mankind, as he lieth with a woman, both of them have committed an abomination: they shall surely be put to death; their blood shall be upon them.*
>
> *Leviticus 20:13*

Again, under the Old Covenant there was no cure for the sin of rebellion; whether it was homosexuality, adultery, or children rebelling against their parents. In the Old Testament, death was often the punishment for such rebellion. It was a way of getting the destructive behavior out of society in the same manner that a doctor cuts a cancerous tumor out of the body. It was done to prevent further spread throughout society and total separation from God. But we live under the New Covenant now, and faith in Jesus is the cure for all sin. We can be forgiven for things for which Old Covenant believers did not receive forgiveness.

> *Be it known unto you therefore, men and brethren, that through this man is preached unto you the forgiveness of sins: And by him all that believe are justified from all things, from which ye could not be justified by the law of Moses.*
>
> *Acts 13:38-39*

God isn't striking people down for sin anymore, but sin is still wrong. Sin is deadly, you shouldn't indulge in it—and homosexuality is a sin. Scripture actually calls it the act of a dog (Deuteronomy 23:17-18).

As I said, I am not against people who are caught up in homosexuality, but I am against the sin. Scripture says it is ungodly, and Christians don't need to make apologies for having the same opinion as God. People engaged in homosexuality are perverting God's creation, and He hates it. He doesn't hate the individuals. He loves them so much that He died in their place and took the punishment for homosexuality. Gay people are forgiven, but God still hates the sin because He knows how damaging it is.

The reason homosexuals are pushing so hard to be accepted by society is because, in their hearts, they know homosexuality is wrong (Romans 1:18-21). They might say they don't feel any guilt because they have always been gay, but it isn't true. I believe God's Word more than what they say (Romans 3:4).

Every time you disobey your conscience, you put a little distance between you and God. By choosing sin, you push God away, and every time you step away from your intuitive knowledge of what is right, you put a layer of insensitivity between you and the Lord. Eventually, you can become so insensitive that it's like your conscience has been seared by a hot iron (1 Timothy 4:2). This is what the Bible calls being reprobate—no longer under conviction of sin. But homosexuality isn't the first step someone takes on the road to being completely insensitive to God; it's one of the last.

The hardening of your heart is a progressive process. It starts by not glorifying what God has done for you, then you move to not being thankful, and finally your thoughts and imagination begin to work against you (Romans 1:21). At that point, you have begun a downward spiral through choices and actions that make you more and more insensitive to God. After which Scripture says,

> *Wherefore God also gave them up to uncleanness through the lusts of their own hearts, to dishonour their own bodies between themselves: Who changed the truth of God into a lie, and worshipped and served the creature more than the Creator, who is blessed for ever. Amen.*
>
> *Romans 1:24-25*

Idolatry isn't just falling down to worship a statue. You can worship money or any other number of things. Covetousness is idolatry (Colossians 3:5), so physical possessions can become your god if you worship them. Everything in the media and pop culture is geared toward creating covetousness inside of you. It is the average condition of people today, and the Bible calls it idolatry.

> *For this cause God gave them up unto vile affections: for even their women did change the natural use into that which is against nature: And likewise also the men, leaving the natural use of the woman, burned in their lust one toward another; men with men working that which is unseemly, and receiving in themselves that recompence of their error which was meet.*
>
> *Romans 1:26-27*

I don't think it is inferring too much to say that the recompense spoken of here is the damaging effects of AIDS and other sexually transmitted diseases. Not that God sent those diseases as punishment. God created laws to govern the earth, and ignoring those natural laws has consequences. If you jump off a bridge, you are going to fall. Likewise, sexually transmitted diseases are the natural result of sexual perversion. Then the Scripture says,

> *And even as they did not like to retain God in their knowledge,*
> *God gave them over to a reprobate mind, to do those things*
> *which are not convenient.*

Romans 1:28

This is saying that God withdrew conviction from people who didn't want Him around. Jesus said that no one goes to the Father unless the Spirit draws them (John 6:44). It is not human nature to seek God, He has to draw us, and people can go so far in their rebellion against Him that God eventually stops trying to draw them to Himself. When that happens, a person becomes reprobate—he has no knowledge of the truth, and he doesn't care. (Don't worry, if you are afraid that you might be reprobate, then you aren't. Any desire to be right with God means that He is still drawing you into relationship with Him. So if you desire relationship with God, you're not reprobate.)

I think we have a lot of reprobate people today who just don't care about God or what He thinks. Hitler bragged, "I have six divisions of SS men absolutely indifferent in matters of religion. It doesn't prevent them from going to death with serenity in their souls." But their serenity wasn't proof they had nothing to fear, it was an indication that they were reprobate. Their conscience was seared as with a hot iron. As soon as they died, I guarantee you they were wishing they hadn't been so indifferent. Unfortunately, we see those kinds of people rising to positions of leadership in businesses and politics all over the world today.

> *Being filled with all unrighteousness, fornication, wickedness, covetousness, maliciousness; full of envy, murder, debate, deceit, malignity; whisperers, Backbiters, haters of God, despiteful, proud, boasters, inventors of evil things, disobedient to parents, Without understanding, covenantbreakers, without natural affection, implacable, unmerciful: Who knowing the judgment of God, that they which commit such things are worthy of death, not only do the same, but have pleasure in them that do them.*
>
> *Romans 1:29-32*

Some of these things are not only allowed, but encouraged in our society. Yet they are all listed as wrong behaviors that move a person toward becoming reprobate. This is the list in which homosexuality finds itself. It is a sin, and it's one of the very last sins in a progression of things that move us away from God toward becoming reprobate. You don't want to go there, and anyone who is practicing homosexuality is flirting with pushing God away for good. The apostle Paul wrote,

> *Know ye not that the unrighteous shall not inherit the kingdom of God? Be not deceived: neither fornicators, nor idolaters, nor adulterers, nor effeminate, nor abusers of themselves*

with mankind, Nor thieves, nor covetous, nor drunkards, nor revilers, nor extortioners, shall inherit the kingdom of God.

1 Corinthians 6:9-10

The phrase translated "abusers of themselves with mankind" is the Greek word *arsenokoitēs,* and it means a sodomite, a homosexual, or "one who lies with a male as with a female." This scripture specifically states that homosexuals will not inherit the kingdom of God. Other scriptures also clearly condemn homosexuality:

Knowing this, that the law is not made for a righteous man, but for the lawless and disobedient, for the ungodly and for sinners, for unholy and profane, for murderers of fathers and murderers of mothers, for manslayers, For whoremongers, for them that defile themselves with mankind, for menstealers, for liars, for perjured persons, and if there be any other thing that is contrary to sound doctrine.

1 Timothy 1:9-10

Even as Sodom and Gomorrha, and the cities about them in like manner, giving themselves over to fornication, and going after strange flesh, are set forth for an example, suffering the vengeance of eternal fire.

Jude 1:7

And turning the cities of Sodom and Gomorrha into ashes condemned them with an overthrow, making them an ensample unto those that after should live ungodly.

2 Peter 2:6

It simply is not possible to read the Bible and think that God approves of homosexuality. God forgives homosexuals because Jesus has already paid the debt, but the act of homosexuality is wrong. It's one thing for a person to know that homosexuality is wrong and to persist in it anyway, but it's something else to try to twist the Gospel into saying that homosexuality is normal behavior, or that it can't be helped.

God would be unjust to command a person not to do something they are genetically disposed toward doing. God doesn't make demands like that. When God tells you not to lie or steal, it's because you have the ability to avoid those behaviors. It would be unreasonable for God to say, "Stop being a man." You can't help the way you were created. But God never created anybody to be a homosexual. Even pro-gay organizations like the APA are admitting that homosexuality is not genetic. Being gay is a choice, just like lying or stealing.

God has never made anyone to be different than the gender they were at birth. If you are a man, then God intends for you to have sexual relations with a woman, and if you are a woman, then God intends for you to have sexual relations with a man. He doesn't make people any other way. The good news for anyone struggling with homosexuality is that you can be set free from the lies that have brought you to that place. You don't have to live under that burden anymore. God loves you, and He has already paid the price to deliver you from that lifestyle.

Chapter 12
Facts and Statistics Regarding Homosexuality

The gay lobby tries to present homosexuality as a completely normal lifestyle. They want you to believe that homosexuals are just like everybody else—aside from their choice in sexual partners—but homosexuality is not normal.

One of the tactics the gay lobby has used to promote the normalcy of homosexuality is to claim a greater occurrence of homosexuality in the population than is true. The gay lobby used to claim that 10% of the population was homosexual. Those faulty figures were taken from a study published in 1948 by a zoologist named Alfred Kinsey, and his study has since been widely criticized for using an unbalanced number of college students and convicted sex offenders. More accurate studies have shown that only 1-2% of Americans claim to be gay, and according to the 2000 US Census Bureau, less than 1% of American households are homosexual—a far lower rate of occurrence than the gay lobby wants the public to believe.

Homosexuality isn't just unusual and immoral—it's harmful. Consider the following facts:[46]

- 43% of white male homosexuals have sex with 500 or more partners in their lifetime.

- 28% of white male homosexuals have over 1,000 sex partners in their lifetime.

It is not normal to have sex with 500 to 1,000 different people, yet that is the case for almost half of the homosexuals in this study. This is a perversion by anyone's standards. That kind of rampant promiscuity explains why homosexual males report far less sexual fidelity than do heterosexuals.[47]

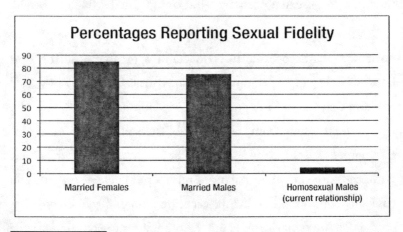

[46] A.P. Bell and M.S. Weinberg, *Homosexualities: A Study of Diversity Among Men and Women* (New York: Simon and Schuster, 1978), 308-309.
[47] Edward Laumann, John H. Gagnon, Robert T. Michael, and Stuart Michaels, *The Social Organization of Sexuality* (Chicago: University of Chicago Press, 1994), 216.
David P. McWhirter and Andrew W. Mattison, *The Male Couple: How Relationships Develop* (Saddle River: Prentice Hall, 1984), 252-253.
Michael W. Wiederman, "Extramarital Sex: prevalence and correlates in a national survey," *Journal of Sex Research*, Vol. 34, no. 2 (1997): 170.

These statistics reveal that homosexuality is a sexual perversion; it's a lifestyle that is directly linked to promiscuity and unfaithfulness. Gay couples aren't just like heterosexual couples; the differences are vast. A study in the Netherlands, where gay marriage has been legal since 2001, revealed that "committed" male homosexual couples had eight sexual partners outside of their relationship every year.[48] Nobody would consider a heterosexual couple normal if they were sleeping with a new person every six weeks in addition to their spouse.

Somebody will object saying that they know a homosexual couple who has been faithfully committed for over 20 years, but that is far and away the rare exception—as these studies show.

On May 8, 2012, North Carolina passed a constitutional amendment that defined marriage solely as the union between a man and a woman. North Carolina's amendment passed 61% to 39%, making them the 30th state to adopt that position. In spite of the majority of states and Americans showing their opposition to gay marriage, President Barack Obama came out the very next day in full support of gay marriage. He cited friends and members of his own staff, "who are in incredibly committed monogamous relationships, same-sex relationships, who are raising kids together..."[49]

---

[48] "Study finds gay unions brief," *The Washington Times*, July 11, 2003. http://www.washingtontimes.com/news/2003/jul/11/20030711-121254-3711r/?page=all#pagebreak (accessed July 12, 2011)

[49] Sam Stein, "Obama Backs Gay Marriage," *The Huffington Post*, May 9, 2012. http://www.huffingtonpost.com/2012/05/09/obama-gay-marriage_n_1503245.html (accessed June 10, 2012)

It might be possible that the individuals the president was talking about were in monogamous homosexual relationships, but if that is true, it would certainly be the exception rather than the rule. This is comparable to endorsing drunk driving because someone you know did it and got home safely without hurting anyone. That does happen, but we justly have laws against driving while under the influence because it's dangerous.

The average homosexual relationship lasts 1½ years, and 95% of the couples in a relationship lasting longer than five years have an open agreement to engage in outside sexual relationships.[50] By comparison, almost 50% of heterosexual marriages last more than 20 years.

Source: National Center for Health Statistics Center for Disease Control and Prevention 2001 and the 2003-2004 Gay/Lesbian Consumer Online Census

---

[50] Ibid.

Partner violence is also much higher in homosexual relationships. Among lesbians, the partner abuse rate is 44 times greater than in heterosexual relationships. Among gay men, the rate at which males are abused by their partners is 300 times greater. Those rates of violence are extremely abnormal. It simply isn't true that homosexual relationships are just like heterosexual marriages with the exception of being same-sex unions. Homosexuality is a vastly different lifestyle.

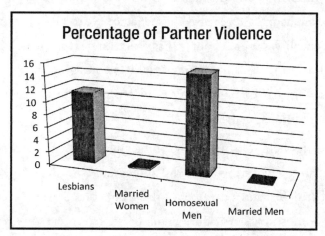

Sources: "Extent, Nature and Consequences of Intimate Partner Violence," U.S. Department of Justice: Office of Justice Programs, July 2000, 30; "Intimate Partner Violence," Bureau of Justice Statistics Special Report, http://bjs.ojp.usdoj.gov/index.cfm?ty=tp&tid=971.

In addition to being sexually and physically harmful, a study performed in England found that homosexuals are at least 50% more likely to suffer from depression, anxiety, and substance abuse.[51] If it were anything else causing that kind of increased risk,

---

[51] "Gays more prone to depression," *Health 24*, September 12, 2008 http://www. health24.com/news/Depression/1-903,47941.asp (accessed July 13, 2011)

the government would be trying to regulate or ban the behavior. I just don't see how you can ignore the dangers associated with homosexuality. It is a destructive lifestyle.

A separate study published in the medical journal *BMC Psychiatry* noted that the risk of suicide jumped over 200% for individuals who had engaged in a homosexual lifestyle. Again, the logical thing to do when you identify a behavior that causes such a dramatic jump in suicides is to warn people not to engage in the behavior. But because the behavior we're talking about is homosexuality, no one wants to say anything. It's not politically correct. In fact, our schools are actually encouraging the behavior by teaching that homosexuality is an acceptable lifestyle alternative to traditional marriage.

In Massachusetts, the father of a kindergartner was arrested and taken to jail during a scheduled meeting with the elementary school principal and a member of the school board over objections to the homosexual curriculum being presented in his son's *kindergarten* class.[52] Even though Massachusetts has a law that allows parents to opt their children out of curriculum they don't approve of, the education authorities in Lexington refused to allow parents to opt their kids out of the homosexual classes. In that school, the gay lobby interpreted the passage of the same-sex marriage law in Massachusetts as a go-ahead to indoctrinate vulnerable kids

---

[52] "Lexington, Mass., father of 6-year-old arrested, spends night in jail over objections to homosexual curriculum in son's kindergarten class," *Mass Resistance*, October 20, 2005. http://www.article8.org/docs/news_events/parker/main.htm accessed July 13, 2011.

into their destructive worldview—regardless of whether or not the parents approved. Such propaganda has no place in the classroom of five- and six-year olds. It's a case of the world calling evil good, and good (the father trying to protect his son) evil (Isaiah 5:20).

The homosexual community is pressing for recognition of their civil unions, claiming that not doing so is discrimination. But what about the religious rights of Christians like this father? If civil unions are legalized and granted protected status, then churches will be forced by law to violate their religious convictions and perform marriages between homosexuals, or be forced to hire homosexuals and grant spousal rights to their partners.

Someone might be yelling, "That's not what would happen," but it has already happened, as with this father in Massachusetts. Churches have already been sued for refusing to allow homosexual marriages in their facilities in states where homosexuals have been granted protected status.[53] Religious organizations have been forced to close rather than violate their moral convictions and treat homosexuality as normal behavior.[54]

Many increased health risks are also associated with homosexuality. Males who adopt a homosexual lifestyle have a 30% greater

---

[53] Ben Johnson, "Judge Rules Christians facility cannot ban same-sex civil union ceremony on its own premises," *LifeSiteNews.com*, January 13, 2012. http://www.lifesitenews.com/news/judge-rules-christian-facility-cannot-ban-same-sex-civil-union-ceremony-on/ (accessed August 24, 2012).

[54] "Catholic Adoption Agency Forced to Close," *The Church of St. Catherine of Siena*, July 24, 2012. http://stcatherinenyc.org/2012/07/24/catholic-adoption-agency-forced-close/ (accessed August 24, 2012).

chance of dying or contracting HIV by age 30,[55] and the overall life expectancy of gay men is 20 years less than heterosexual men.[56] Data as of 1989 showed the rates of anal cancer in male homosexual practitioners to be 10 times that of heterosexual males, and growing.[57] For those with AIDS, the rates are doubled.[58]

Lesbians are at higher risk for certain gynecologic cancers, and they are more than twice as likely as straight women to be obese— which is associated with higher rates of cancer and heart disease. Gay men are twice as likely to have been diagnosed with, and then survived, cancer, and they are at higher risk for anal, lung, testicular and immune-system cancers.[59] Experts also believe that lesbians are more likely to get breast cancer than heterosexual women. The list of health risks seems never-ending. Here is a summary of what we've mentioned so far:

---

[55] Tom McFeely, "What About the Children? American College of Pediatricians Warns Against Same-Sex Families," *National Catholic Register,* June 3, 2008. http://www.ncregister.com/site/article/15089 (accessed July 14, 2011).
[56] John R. Diggs Jr. MD, "The Health Risks of Gay Sex," *Catholic Education Resource Center,* 2002. http://www.catholiceducation.org/articles/homosexuality/ho0075.html (accessed July 14, 2011).
[57] Mads Melbye, Charles Rabkin, et al., "Changing patterns of anal cancer incidence in the United States, 1940-1989," *American Journal of Epidemiology* (New York: Oxford University Press, 1994), 139: 772-780, p. 779, Table 2.
[58] James Goedert, et al., for the AIDS-Cancer Match Study Group, "Spectrum of AIDS-associated malignant disorders," *The Lancet* (New York: Elsevier, 1998), 351: 1833-1839, p. 1836
[59] Randy Dotinga, "Gay men face a higher risk of anal, lung, testicular and immune-system cancers," *U.S. News & World Report,* May 9, 2011. http://health.usnews.com/health-news/family-health/cancer/articles/2011/05/09/gay-men-more-likely-to-have-had-cancer (accessed July 14, 2011).

- Partner violence is 44 times greater among lesbians and 300 times greater among homosexual men

- Homosexuals are at least 50% more likely to suffer from depression, anxiety, and substance abuse

- The risk of suicide is 200% greater for homosexuals

- Homosexuals are twice as likely to contract AIDS

- Life expectancy is reduced by 20 years among homosexuals

- Homosexual men are twice as likely to have been diagnosed with cancer

- Lesbians are at a higher risk for breast cancer

- Lesbians are twice as likely to be obese

The Surgeon General puts warnings on cigarettes because they have been shown to reduce life expectancy by ten years. Homosexuality is twice as deadly as cigarettes, by those standards. It is not the normal, healthy lifestyle that the gay lobby wants everyone to believe it is. If people were not "Politically Correct phobic," they would put warnings out about the dangers of homosexuality.

As these statistics show, homosexuality isn't just morally wrong—it is a hugely destructive behavior. God doesn't want people getting hurt or destroying their lives by getting caught up in this. It is important to talk about the dangers because homosexuality is a choice, and you can avoid the consequences by avoiding the behavior. I'm not being hateful by applying my Christian philosophy to point out the dangers of the homosexual lifestyle any more than the Surgeon General is being mean by putting warning labels on cigarettes. I'm trying to save people from being deceived and from getting hurt. The good news is that anyone practicing homosexuality can get out of that lifestyle. No one is destined to be gay.

I have had people working in my ministry and attending my Bible college who have been delivered from the homosexual lifestyle. By their own testimony, they had serious problems at one time, but now they are completely free. They are happier than they have ever been, and they are totally liberated from homosexual tendencies. Contrary to what many people have been told, homosexuality is not genetic. It is not the way God made you. No matter how trapped you might feel, Jesus can save you out of that lifestyle.

It is not only okay for Christians to employ their Christian philosophy and speak out against homosexuality, it is imperative that we do, because the truth is what sets people free (John 8:32). Scripture is clear that no one engaging in a homosexual lifestyle will inherit the kingdom of God, and homosexuals won't know that God has a better, healthier, and more fulfilling plan for their lives unless someone tells them. You shouldn't be mean about it; truth shouldn't be used like a club to beat people into submission. But as long as your motivation is love, I encourage you to speak the truth and not to be afraid of being criticized.

Chapter 13

Abortion

On a Monday morning in July, when the Colorado House of Representatives was celebrating the 90th anniversary of Planned Parenthood, a young woman took the floor to sing the national anthem. As an advocate for people with cerebral palsy, the House was honored to have her sing for them. The woman's emotionally engaging performance had the entire chamber singing along with her at one point. After a stirring round of applause, one of the representatives stood to tell the young woman's story—and the mood in the chamber suddenly changed.

The young woman was Gianna Jessen, survivor of a saline abortion performed at a Planned Parenthood clinic in California, and her cerebral palsy was caused by the saline injected into her mother's womb. She was invited, the representative said, to put a face on the celebration of Planned Parenthood. The majority leader behind the celebration felt like they had been manipulated, and was later quoted as saying, "I think it was amazingly rude to use a human being as an example of personal politics."[60] Yet abor-

---

[60] Ted Harvey, "Planned Parenthood Celebration Jolted by Abortion Survivor," *Catholic Education Resource Center*, 2006. http://catholiceducation. org/articles/abortion/ab0107.htm (accessed August 24, 2012).

tion is precisely about human beings, not politics. It's about all the people who never get a chance to live and to sing.

The medical professionals who perform the abortions have billions of dollars worth of incentives to harden their hearts against the human crisis that plays out before them every day. But if those choosing abortion could see the human pain, suffering and death they are causing, any rational person would realize this is wrong.

Many who support abortion try to dehumanize babies living in their mothers' wombs by pretending that babies are just a mass of tissue until the moment of birth, but we know that isn't true. Everything needed for life is already present in our reproductive cells, and human development begins immediately after the male and female reproductive cells meet. In other words, babies are living human beings from the moment of conception. In the Psalms it says,

> For thou hast possessed my reins: thou hast covered me in my mother's womb. I will praise thee; for I am fearfully and wonderfully made: marvellous are thy works; and that my soul knoweth right well. My substance was not hid from thee, when I was made in secret, and curiously wrought in the lowest parts of the earth. Thine eyes did see my substance, yet being unperfect; and in thy book all my members were written, which in continuance were fashioned, when as yet there was none of them.
>
> *Psalm 139:13–16*

Abortion

The NIV translates these verses as, "For you created my inmost being; you knit me together in my mother's womb. I praise you because I am fearfully and wonderfully made; your works are wonderful, I know that full well. My frame was not hidden from you when I was made in the secret place. When I was woven together in the depths of the earth, your eyes saw my unformed body. All the days ordained for me were written in your book before one of them came to be.

The Amplified Bible says, "For You did form my inward parts; You did knit me together in my mother's womb. I will confess *and* praise You *for You are fearful and wonderful and* for the awful wonder of my birth! Wonderful are Your works, and that my inner self knows right well. My frame was not hidden from You when I was being formed in secret [and] intricately *and* curiously wrought [as if embroidered with various colors] in the depths of the earth [a region of darkness and mystery]. Your eyes saw my unformed substance, and in Your book all the days [of my life] were written before ever they took shape, when as yet there was none of them."

God knows unborn children while they are still in their mothers' wombs. He knows us long before we are completely developed; while we are still a developing cell being "made in secret." God knows everything about how you will look when you are just an embryo. He knows your hair color, your eye color, how tall you will be. He knows absolutely everything, and He has already recorded everything about you in His book.

When someone has an abortion, they aren't just destroying a hunk of tissue. Abortion kills a living person known by God, a person whose features and characteristics have already been written down by God. Abortion destroys human beings into whom God has breathed life.

Abortion isn't a matter of *"choice,"* as pro-abortionists want to spin it. No one has the right to kill an infant. Abortion is murder, and it's wrong. I'm not saying this to hurt anyone, but you can't fix a problem until you identify it, so we need to be clear about the abortion crisis in our society. God has already provided forgiveness for anyone who has had an abortion, so I'm not reproaching anyone. I'm condemning the practice of abortion. No one should be given the freedom to kill a child. It's not right, and we need to stand against it.

The story behind Roe v. Wade, the famous Supreme Court case that legalized abortion in 1973, is an interesting one. The real name of the woman called "Jane Roe" in the case is Norma McCorvey. In 1973, she had one small child and was pregnant with her second when she was chosen to be the plaintiff in the suit. She says she was worried about being able to take care of two small children and wanted to get a legal abortion, but Norma never actually had an abortion. In fact, today, she is the mother of three daughters and is a pro-life activist who says her involvement in Roe v. Wade was the worst mistake of her life.

Roe v. Wade was based on a "woman's personal right to privacy and to choice." The justices rationalized their decision by saying that an unborn child is not a living person, and so the child doesn't have legal rights that are protected by the state (like the right to life). This is not true—it's just the only logic they could come up with to legally justify abortion. We all know that an unborn child is a living human being, and science has since proven it.

In 1973, there wasn't definite scientific proof that an embryo was a child. People hadn't questioned whether that was so. It was just commonly accepted that an unborn child was human. But in the absence of "scientific" research on this matter, the Supreme Court ruled that an unborn child was not a separate human and therefore, the woman had a right to choose what to do with her own body. Although science has since proven that argument wrong, the practice continues.

Abortion shouldn't be about a woman's privacy or her right to control her future. It's about the life of an unborn child—life that should be protected. No one has the right to take the life of another; especially the innocent life of a child.

Scripture clearly shows that unborn babies are living human beings. After the angel Gabriel announced to Mary that she would conceive a child by the power of the Holy Spirit, Mary went to visit her older cousin Elisabeth who was also pregnant at the time. Elisabeth was pregnant with John the Baptist, and Scripture says he leapt for joy in Elisabeth's womb when Mary entered the room—which means that he was experiencing emotion as an unborn six-month-old baby.

...when Elisabeth heard the salutation of Mary, the babe leaped in her womb; and Elisabeth was filled with the Holy Ghost: And she spake out with a loud voice, and said, Blessed art thou among women, and blessed is the fruit of thy womb. And whence is this to me, that the mother of my Lord should come to me? For, lo, as soon as the voice of thy salutation sounded in mine ears, the babe leaped in my womb for joy.

Luke 1:41–44

Under the New Covenant, the Holy Spirit comes upon us and He never leaves us, but it was exceptional to be filled with the Holy Spirit before Jesus ascended into heaven and the Father sent the Holy Spirit to abide with us forever. The Holy Spirit would come upon people to help them perform a specific task, but He didn't dwell in them continuously.

However, it was prophesied that John the Baptist would be filled with the Holy Spirit from his mother's womb (Luke 1:15), and the scripture above records the moment it happened—when he was still an unborn baby. The key point here is that the Holy Spirit doesn't fill inanimate tissue. He only fills living human beings. For John the Baptist to be filled with the Holy Spirit in his mother's womb proves that unborn babies are distinct human beings in God's eyes.

The relative maturity of a baby doesn't determine whether or not he or she is a living human person. A baby doesn't have to be ready to care for herself outside of the womb in order to be considered "alive." God designed babies to grow and mature in the womb. Even after babies are born, you still have to feed and care for them. You have to protect babies, feed them, and provide them with the right environment and temperature. Infants can't survive outside the womb on their own because it takes several years for children to mature enough to be able to take care of themselves.

Developmental stages are just measurements of maturity—they don't indicate the beginning of life—whether the person is one day, fourteen months, or thirty years old. A baby's life doesn't begin at some arbitrary stage of development—babies are living people from the very moment of conception.

Jeremiah was ordained to be a prophet from his mother's womb, as was Isaiah. This truth was only highlighted in scripture for a few individuals, but God is not a respecter of persons (Acts 10:34). He treats us all the same, which means that God knows everyone from the earliest stages of development. Even when you were being formed in the womb, God knew you and had already fashioned a purpose for you.

> *Then the word of the LORD came unto me, saying, Before I formed thee in the belly I knew thee; and before thou camest forth out of the womb I sanctified thee, and I ordained thee a prophet unto the nations.*
>
> *Jeremiah 1:4-5*

Here again, this scripture says that God "knew" Jeremiah when he was still in the womb, which shows that God views a fetus as a person—not mere tissue. (I hate to use the term "fetus" to refer to an unborn human being, but I want to make sure those who do use that term get the point that what they call a "fetus" is a living human being.) The Apostle Paul also said that he was separated to preach the Gospel of Jesus Christ when he was still in his mother's womb (Galatians 1:15). These examples demonstrate how the Lord knows each of us from the earliest stages of development, and He puts gifts and life-purpose in us long before we are born.

Even though unborn babies are dependent upon their mothers while they are developing in the womb during pregnancy, God views babies as unique persons from the moment of conception. In God's eyes, a fetus is a living human being, and taking the life of an unborn baby is no different than taking the life of any other human being. The majority of society may not view it that way, and the United States Supreme Court may not agree, but Scripture says, "let God be true, but every man a liar" (Romans 3:4). In other words, it really doesn't matter what everyone else is saying. God says babies are living human beings from the moment of conception, and His Word is true.

This is what the whole debate on abortion comes down to: Is the baby a human being from the moment of conception, or not? The answer is yes, an unborn baby is a living human being, and once life is conceived, you don't have the right to end it by abortion. It's not a matter of choice, or convenience.

Pro-abortion supporters are trying to say that abortion is about a woman's right to choose whether or not she wants be a mother and raise a child—totally ignoring the fact that abortion ends a life no one has the right to take. A woman who becomes pregnant is already a mother, so anyone who wants to exercise their right to "choose," should choose not to have sexual intercourse until they are ready to have a child.

As a society, we have been lied to. We've been told that abortion is only about a woman's right to choose, but that isn't true. Even if you don't consider the Scriptural evidence, medical science has shown that an unborn baby has a beating heart within the first month of pregnancy. This means that within two to three weeks of conception—before the mother even realizes she is pregnant—the baby is already a separate human being.[61] It isn't accurate to claim that abortion is about a woman's right to choose what happens to her own body because unborn babies are not part of their mothers' bodies—they are separate individuals.

I'm certain people would feel a lot differently about abortion if they could see the fingernails, eyes, feet, hands, and delicate details of the aborted babies. Seeing those pictures, you know instinctively that unborn babies are not just hunks of flesh; they are viable human beings who should be given the chance to develop and become the people God wants them to be.

---

[61] American Congress of Obstetricians and Gynecologists, "How Your Baby Grows During Pregnancy," Last modified August 2011. http://www.acog.org/For_Patients
Linda Hinkle, "When Does An Unborn Baby Have A Heartbeat?" *Live STRONG.com*, June 14, 2011. http://www.livestrong.com/article/242600-when-does-an-unborn-baby-have-a-heartbeat/#ixzz1cZPN5lx0 (accessed August 24, 2012).

I don't think most people realize how quickly unborn babies take on mature characteristics. Scripture says that "the life of the flesh is in the blood," so just the fact that a baby's heart begins to pump its own blood within weeks of conception is a revealing truth (Leviticus 17:11). Here are some other developmental milestones:[62]

- Day 22: The baby's heart begins to beat with the child's own blood, often a different type than the mother's.

- Week 3: The child's backbone, spinal column, and nervous system are forming. The liver, kidneys and intestines begin to take shape.

- Week 4: The child is ten thousand times larger than the original fertilized egg.

- Week 5: Eyes, legs, and hands begin to develop.

See fetus at 5 weeks- Eyes, legs and hands develop. (Fig.15) pg. 199.

- Week 6: Brain waves are detectable; mouth and lips are present; fingernails are forming.

- Week 7: Eyelids, toes, and a distinct nose form. The baby is kicking and swimming.

- Week 8: Every organ is in place, bones begin to replace cartilage, and fingerprints begin to form. The baby also begins to hear.

---

[62] National Right to Life, "Fetal development from conception to birth," Last modified January 7, 2003. http://www.nrlc.org/abortion/facts/fetaldevelopment.html

- Weeks 9 and 10: Teeth begin to form, fingernails develop. The baby can turn his head, frown, and hiccup.

- Week 10: The baby can "breathe" amniotic fluid and urinate.

- Week 11: The baby can grasp objects placed in his hand; all organ systems are functioning. The baby has a skeletal structure, nerves, and circulation.

- Week 12: The baby has all of the parts necessary to experience pain, including nerves, spinal cord, and thalamus. Vocal cords are complete. The baby can suck his or her thumb.

- Week 14: At this age, the heart pumps several quarts of blood through the body every day.

- Week 15: The baby has an adult's taste buds.

- Month 4: Bone Marrow is now beginning to form. The heart is pumping 25 quarts of blood a day. By the end of month 4, the baby will be 8-10 inches in length and will weigh up to half a pound.

- Week 17: The baby can have dream (REM) sleep.

Week 17- Baby can have REM sleep. (Fig.16) on page 200.

- Week 20: The baby recognizes her mother's voice. (This is also the earliest stage at which partial birth abortions are performed).

I don't see how anyone can look at these scientifically documented developmental stages and still try to claim that unborn
babies are merely a part of the mother's body—and it's her choice
whether or not the baby should live. No, unborn babies are separate, living human beings who have as much a right to life as any
other living person. You can't argue that the baby is a part of the
mother's body—unborn babies have their own blood type, finger
prints, feelings, brain waves, dreams, and all sorts of things we
know are unique to individuals.

The women who go to abortion clinics aren't told any of this,
but I think they would feel differently about abortion if they were.
I think more people would see that abortion is not a matter of a
woman's choice—it's about the right of an unborn child to live
and fulfill God's creative purposes. There is not a civilized country
on the face of the earth that gives any woman the freedom of
choice to kill another person. Unborn babies are human beings,
and nobody has the right to take those children's lives.

The abortion rate in the United States is alarming: 3,600
abortions are performed every day, which amounts to more than
1.3 million abortions every year—or one every 24 seconds. Since
Roe v. Wade legalized abortion in the United States in 1973, 54.3
million babies have been aborted.[63] (This is the total at the end of
2011, but with 3,600 babies being killed by abortion every day,
the total continues to grow at a frightening pace. These staggering

---

[63] "Facts on Induced Abortion in the United States," *The Guttmacher
Institute*, web, http://www.guttmacher.org/pubs/fb_induced_abortion.
html

42% OF ALL **YEARLY** DEATHS IN THE WORLD ARE FROM ABORTION

57 Million Other Deaths

42 Million Abortion Deaths

A Worldwide Crisis

© 2010 Abortion Blackout, LLC. Source: Alan Guttmacher Institute, World Health Organization, Causes of Death

Despite all of the evidence proving that an unborn baby is a living human being, a lot of people aren't letting facts get in the way of what they believe. Abortion is accepted in our society, and some people are going to support it, no matter what evidence you show them. In many ways, our society has become numb to the truth—which is that no matter what the circumstances are or how inconvenient the birth of a child might be, there is no justification for abortion.

We often hear abortion supporters defending the practice of abortion as a necessary option in so-called "hard cases" involving rape, incest, or medical issues. I'll get to those issues in just a moment, but first I think we should keep in mind that rape, incest, and medical issues only account for 6% of all abortions—that's a very small percentage. Recent research shows women give the following reasons for getting an abortion:[65]

---

[64] "Abortion Facts," *Abortion Blackout*, web, http://www.abortionblackout. com/abortion-facts?page=3

[65] Lawrence B. Finer, et al, "Reasons U.S. Women Have Abortions: Quantitative and Qualitative Perspectives," *The Guttmacher Institute*,

- 74% said having a baby would interfere with their career, education, or ability to care for other family members

- 73% say they couldn't afford a baby

- 48% don't want to be single mothers, or are having relationship problems

- 25% don't want anyone else to know they have had sex or are pregnant

- 1% were the victims of rape

- less than .5% became pregnant as the result of incest

The women involved in this study obviously gave multiple reasons for having an abortion, which is why the percentages don't add up to 100. But when all of the responses were examined, the study revealed that 92% of women have abortions for social or "other" reasons. Not only that, but of the less than 6% who cited medical reasons, researchers thought many of those women seemed to be giving their own opinion, such as morning sickness, rather than indicating a life-threatening condition or diagnosis by a medical doctor.[66] In any case, the vast majority of women admit to having abortions for the sake of convenience.

"Hard case" abortions raise some difficult issues, but they are still not a justification for abortion. To say that abortion is justified in cases where the child might be born with physical or mental

---

web, http://www.guttmacher.org/pubs/journals/3711005.pdf
[66] Randall K. O'Bannon, Ph.D., "New Study Examines Reasons Women Have Abortions," *National Right to Life Center*, web, http://www.nrlc.org/news/2005/NRL10/NewStudy.html

disabilities is just wrong. It gives the impression that the value of human life depends on the health or condition of the person, as if our value is judged by what we can contribute to society—which is nonsense. Young people aren't more valuable than old people, and healthy people aren't more valuable than sick people. And nobody has the right to kill another person because they somehow judge the other person's quality of life to be insufficient.

All human life is equally valuable because we are made in the image of God. It isn't our place to decide who should live or die—even if we learn that an unborn child may have physical or mental handicaps that will make life challenging. The relative health of an unborn baby has no bearing on the fact that he or she is a living human being, and all human beings have the right to live.

History has shown the devastating effects of societies that start deciding who should live and who should die. It is not often discussed, but there is a direct link between the philosophy of evolution and the horrors of Nazism that erupted in Germany. In short, once people began to believe that humans were the result of evolution, they started to wonder which humans were the most evolved and what could be done to breed a better race—and which people should be removed from the gene pool.

Nazism was a philosophical blend of Social Darwinism and eugenics. Social Darwinism was the theory that humans were subject to the same forces of evolution that Darwin proposed for plants and animals. Eugenics was "the study of hereditary improvement of the human race by controlled selective breeding."[67] Eugenicists thought that humans should take the same approach to reproduction that cattle ranchers take to breeding livestock—only breed the strongest and healthiest. Supporters of eugenics believed that Darwin's proposed force of natural selection was moving too slowly and steps needed to be taken toward favoring the best and eliminating the worst. This was the same philosophy behind Hitler's "master race" idea.

It's worth noting that Nazi Germany's first program of systematic murder targeted mentally and physically disabled children living in institutions within Germany or its controlled territories.[68] The sole purpose of the euthanasia program was to kill people the eugenicists believed were not worthy of life. Notably, the Nazi's first victims were infants and toddlers. The fact that they started killing the handicapped two years before they targeted Jews demonstrates that the evil of the Holocaust didn't descend upon Germany overnight; it was a slow steady process. After society turned a blind eye to the killing of the handicapped, the Nazi government was emboldened to begin a more aggressive program of murder: the Holocaust, which killed 6 million Jews.

The eugenics movement in Germany spawned Nazism and resulted in the mass murder of millions of innocent lives, but the eugenics movement in the United States took a different form. The chief proponent of eugenics in the United States was a

---

[67] *New American Dictionary*, s.v. "eugenics."
[68] "Euthanasia Program," *The United States Holocaust Museum*, web, http://www.ushmm.org/wlc/en/article.php?ModuleId=10005200

woman named Margaret Sanger. You may recognize her name: she founded the American Birth Control League in 1928, which later became known as Planned Parenthood. Sanger coined the term "birth control," and she promoted abortion as a way to kill unwanted babies—it was her idea for purifying the gene pool. Quotes from Sanger's writings leave no doubt about her motivations for promoting abortion:

- "We desire to stop at its source the disease, poverty and feeble-mindedness and insanity which exist today, for these lower the standards of civilization and make for race deterioration."[69]

- "…we would make it a law that children should be brought into the world only when they were welcome, invited, and wanted; that they would arrive with a clean bill of health and heritage; that they would possess healthy, happy, well-mated, and mature parents."[70]

- "Every single case of inherited defect, every malformed child, every congenitally tainted human being brought into this world is of infinite importance to that poor individual; but it is of scarcely less importance to the rest

[69] Margaret Sanger, "The Morality of Birth Control," (speech, delivered Nov 18, 1921), web, http://www.americanrhetoric.com/speeches/margarets angermoralityofbirthcontrol.htm

[70] Margaret Sanger, "The Children's Era," (speech, delivered March 1925), web, http://www.americanrhetoric.com/speeches/margaretsanger childrensera.html

of us and to all of our children who must pay in one way or another for these biological and racial mistakes."[71]

- "...the campaign for Birth Control is not merely of eugenic value, but is practically identical in ideal, with the final aims of Eugenics." Sanger concludes, "Birth Control propaganda is thus the entering wedge for the Eugenic educator."[72]

Notice that Sanger believed only "well-mated" parents with a clean bill of health and *heritage* should be allowed to have children. Her ideals were blatantly racist. Among the people whom Sanger thought should not be allowed to procreate were the "...diseased, feeble-minded, and [the] pauper element dependent entirely upon the normal and fit members of society for their support. There is no doubt in the minds of all thinking people that the procreation of this group should be stopped."

For Margaret Sanger and Planned Parenthood, birth control and abortion were all about purifying the human race through controlled and selective breeding. She thought of abortion as a propaganda tool to "weed out" the members of society she deemed unworthy of life.

---

[71] Margaret Sanger, *The Pivot of Civilization*, (New York: Brentano's, 1922). Chapter 12, web, http://digital.library.upenn.edu/webbin/gutbook/lookup?num=1689

[72] Margaret Sanger, "The Eugenic Value of Birth Control Propaganda," *Birth Control Review*, October 1921. http://www.nyu.edu/projects/sanger/webedition/app/documents/show.php?sangerDoc=238946.xml

Abortion

I know abortion is not a fun topic to discuss, but it would be wrong for us to quietly go about our lives, pretending that the horrors of abortion aren't happening. We have a duty to employ our Christian philosophy and speak out for the unborn children who cannot speak for themselves. All you have to do is look at the procedure for partial-birth abortions, or the criminal conditions that have been found in some late-term abortion clinics, to see that abortion devalues human life and desensitizes society to the violence of murder. If you don't already know, I'll describe partial-birth abortion in the least disturbing terms possible. It's a surgical procedure in which the baby is partially removed from the mother's womb, then a doctor punctures the baby's skull and suctions out his or her brain tissue. This is performed on babies 20 weeks old or older.

I don't care how you look at it, partial-birth abortion is murder. Even the thin legal separation between what constitutes a partial-birth abortion and what meets the criteria for murder reveals the fallacy of the argument that abortion is about choice. Babies don't become living human beings after exiting their mother's wombs— they are living people from conception—and the value of human life isn't determined by age.

In fact, a doctor who performed late term abortions at a clinic in Philadelphia is on trial for seven counts of murder because he performed abortions by inducing labor and killing the babies after they were completely out of the womb. See, it's a legal abortion to kill the baby as long as the baby's head is the only body part out of the womb, but if you deliver the rest of the baby's body before performing the procedure, then it's murder. What kind of twisted logic says it's okay to kill a baby in the womb, but it's first degree murder to kill the same baby two seconds later if he or she is completely out of the mother's womb?

We all recognize that it's just as wrong to kill a ten year old as it is to kill a two year old, but abortion supporters try to say that it's okay to kill a baby depending on how old he or she is, or whether the baby is in or out of the womb. It's a totally illogical argument. The stage of development has nothing to do with the value of human life. It's just as wrong to kill a one-day-old baby as it is to perform a partial-birth abortion on a baby while he or she is in the womb, or to kill the baby after it comes out of the womb. Murder is murder, no matter how old the victim is.

It saddens me that 70% of women who have an abortion claim to be Christian at the time of the procedure. As a church, we have failed those women. The only reason I can imagine a Christian supporting abortion is that they don't know the facts. They have bought into the lie that an unborn child isn't truly alive. They have no Christian philosophy by which their life is guided.

Scripture and science both prove that unborn babies *are* living human beings. When Roe v. Wade legalized abortion in 1973, the medical community hadn't completed all of the studies we know about today that prove unborn babies are viable human beings, so the Supreme Court decided to rule that a child in the womb had no rights. But we know better: unborn babies are human beings, and they do have rights.

With current statistics showing that 33% of all women will have had an abortion by age 45, I suspect that most people know someone who has had an abortion. God loves every single one of those women, and He has provided forgiveness for anyone who will accept it, so I'm not trying to condemn anyone who has had an abortion. I'm not mad at anyone, and I'm not trying to hurt or slander anyone. I'm just trying to save lives and show people the importance of having a Christian perspective on abortion. In order to do that, we have to speak openly and honestly about it.

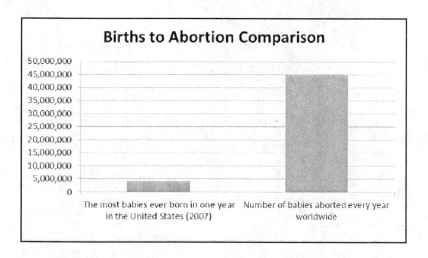

Socially, abortion causes a tremendous loss of human potential in our societies. Worldwide, approximately 125,000 abortions are performed every day—that's more than 42 million abortions every year.[73] To put that number in perspective, the most babies that have ever been born in the United States in one year is 4.3

---

[73] "Abortions in the world," *Worldometers: real-time world statistics*, web, http://www.worldometers.info/abortions/

million,[74] which would mean that for every infant born in the U.S., at least another 10 babies around the world are killed by abortion. Imagine how much potential has been eliminated from our midst. We'll never know how many innovators and leaders have been killed by abortion; how many Martin Luther King, Jrs or Billy Grahams were never given the chance to make our world a better place. Additionally, the effect of abortion on women's health has been awful. Look at these facts:

- Having an abortion can triple a woman's risk of developing breast cancer later in life.[75]

- A study in England found an 80% increase in the rate of breast cancer since 1971, when the number of abortions rose from 18,000 to nearly 200,000 a year.[76]

- Women who have abortions are 30% more likely to develop a mental illness.[77]

- Women who have an abortion are three times as likely to develop drug or alcohol addiction.[78]

---

[74] Dan Glaister, "Number of babies born in the US reaches record levels," *The Guardian*, March 18, 2009. Web. http://www.guardian.co.uk/world/2009/mar/18/birth-rate-us-baby-boomers

[75] Simon Caldwell, "Abortion 'triples breast cancer risk': Fourth study finds terminations linked to disease," *Daily Mail*, June 23, 2010. Web. http://www.dailymail.co.uk/health/article-1288955/Abortion-triple-risk-breast-cancer.html#ixzz1dhsHHeJu

[76] Ibid.

[77] David M. Fergusson, L. John Horwood, and Joseph M. Boden, "Abortion and Mental Health Disorders: Evidence from a 30-year Longitudinal Study," *British Journal of Psychiatry*, December 2008. http://www.physiciansforlife.org/content/view/1681/26/

[78] Ibid.

- Women with a history of induced abortion are at a significantly higher risk for psychiatric problems, adjustment disorders, bipolar disorder, depressive psychosis, neurotic depression, schizophrenia, parenting difficulties, and death from various violent and natural causes.[79]

The health risks associated with abortion are astonishing. There are more risks than I have listed here, but I think this list is long enough for us to see the wide range of dangers associated with abortion. The point is that abortion isn't only wrong from a religious or moral standpoint—it's wrong from every way you can look at it.

---

[79] Priscilla Coleman, Ph.D., "Abortion Mental Health Research: Update and Quality of Evidence," *Association for Intedisciplinary Research in Values and Social Change Research Bulletin*, Spring 2008, Vol. 20, no. 2. http://www.abortionresearch.us/images/Vol20No2.pdf

Chapter 14

In the World, but Not of It

The secular world has basically beat the body of Christ back into the four walls of the church. You can have religious opinions—as long as you keep them to yourself. They don't want Christians saying anything publicly about God or morality, but Christians have as much a right to free speech as anybody. It's okay for Christians to have a philosophy that guides our opinions on current issues, and it's okay for us to express those opinions.

We looked at homosexuality, abortion, and creation from a Christian perspective. We could keep going and discuss a Christian philosophy for marriage, raising children, work ethic, managing money, and every other topic you can think of. Although Scripture has guidance for every situation imaginable, it isn't practical for me to try to present a Christian philosophy for all of them in this book. Instead, I have tried to help establish a way of thinking that will allow you to form a Christian philosophy on your own—regardless of what situation you may be facing.

The world is heading in a different direction than God, so we can't just adopt the popular opinions and beliefs of society. As Christians, we are separate from the world. Our born-again spirits set us apart, and there should be a noticeable difference in the lives and opinions of people who have the life of God in them versus people who have only physical life.

People who have a relationship with God should be different from the world—which represents people who are separated from God. Scripture says that we are in the world, be we are not *of* the world (John 15:19). The Word of God shows us that we live in a hostile environment, and it warns us not to get too comfortable with the world's way of doing things. For example, it tells us:

> *Be ye not unequally yoked together with unbelievers: for what fellowship hath righteousness with unrighteousness? and what communion hath light with darkness?*

> *2 Corinthians 6:14*

This scripture is almost always applied toward marriage and the idea that Christians shouldn't marry unbelievers, which is true, but it isn't limited to that. It also applies to business dealings, friends, and other important relationships in your life. I'm not suggesting Christians should avoid all dealings with unbelievers, but we do need to be careful not to allow the world to influence us.

The world is not embracing Christianity. Jesus plainly told believers that they would be rejected by the world just as He was. Another scripture says that all who live godly in Christ Jesus will be persecuted (2 Timothy 3:12), so the only way to escape persecution from the world is to go with the flow of society. Once you start following God, then you are going to be living contrary to the tendencies of the world, and you will experience opposition at times. Being a Christian is more like swimming upstream than floating along with all of the trends and opinions of society. Even a dead fish can float downstream. It takes backbone to swim against the current.

If you are watching the same television shows and movies as unbelievers, reading the same books and magazines, then you are going to experience some of the same results in your life. When you put garbage in, you're going to get garbage out. Yet the average Christian is fully identified with the world. They pipe the same junk into their lives, and they are living the way the world lives. Scripture says that you will be the way you think in your heart (Proverbs 23:7), which means that thinking like the world will make you look like the world. You may be born again in your spirit, but your life is going to go the way of your dominant thoughts. Scripture says,

> *For to be carnally minded is death; but to be spiritually minded is life and peace.*

> *Romans 8:6*

It doesn't say that being carnally minded tends toward death, or will lead to death for certain types of people. No, it says to be carnally minded is death; they are the same thing. To be spiritually minded, on the other hand, is to be focused on the Word of God. Spiritually minded people are not pressed into the mold of this world; they don't take in all of the same junk through the media, and they don't think like the world.

The world system that surrounds us is hostile to Christians. Living in the world, we need to have the same attitude that scuba divers have when they are underwater. I've only been scuba diving once, and even though I enjoyed it, I knew it was a hostile environment. I couldn't just take off my mask and breathe underwater the same way I breathe on land. I had to take a special approach toward surviving in that environment.

Similarly, this world is not really our home. Christians have been born from above, and although we live and breathe on earth, this is still a hostile environment. If we don't understand that fact and just go about our lives nonchalantly, then the world is going to have greater influence on us. You can't watch television and sitcoms and think that sitcoms present a normal model for living. If you do, then you're going to get caught up in the same casual sex, fighting, and nastiness portrayed in those shows. As Christians, we should be different.

You live in a hostile environment, and if you are just taking it all in the way the rest of society is, then you are being corrupted by the world's way of thinking. We are different from past generations of Christians in that the world's philosophy is being piped into our homes via Internet, television, and radio 24 hours a day. To keep those negative influences from destroying us, we need to have a philosophy that we are in the world but not a part of it, which is exactly what Scripture says:

And what concord hath Christ with Belial? or what part hath he that believeth with an infidel? And what agreement hath the temple of God with idols? for ye are the temple of the living God; as God hath said, I will dwell in them, and walk in them; and I will be their God, and they shall be my people. Wherefore come out from among them, and be ye separate, saith the Lord, and touch not the unclean thing; and I will receive you.

2 Corinthians 6:15-17

This isn't saying that we should hate unbelievers, but we are supposed to treat them differently. For instance, I don't value the opinion of lost people as much as I value what the Word of God says. I don't believe everything an unbeliever tells me; no matter what their credentials are. You can have 32 degrees and still be frozen. I interact with unbelievers, and I don't think being around them defiles me in some way; that's not what I mean. I just don't embrace or accept everything they say.

This scripture is a command from God to come out from among unbelievers. Practically, I don't think this means we are supposed to withdraw into the walls of our churches and completely cut ourselves off from the world. No, we are the salt of the earth, and unless we live in society, we can't season the world. Christians should be in the public arena—running for political office, speaking on television, and publishing newspapers. The separation doesn't need to be physical, but everyone should be able to tell the difference between Christians and unbelievers. One of the very first scriptures that God spoke to me says,

And be not conformed to this world: but be ye transformed by the renewing of your mind, that ye may prove what is that good, and acceptable, and perfect, will of God.

Romans 12:2

The Greek word translated *conformed* in this scripture means "poured into the mold of." As you go through life, it has a way of heating up and melting you. You don't reach old age with the same opinions and perspective you had when you were young. Things happen, and you lose the naiveté of youth. Yet, in a sense, you get to pick the mold that you are conformed to—but it takes effort, and you need to focus on the truth in God's Word. Otherwise, you'll be poured into the mold of the world, and you will end up being conformed to the world's way of thinking.

People with a worldly philosophy don't like it when Christians disagree with them, so speaking the truth inevitably brings persecution. Jesus spoke the truth and the world killed Him for it. Just like the world persecuted Jesus, it will use criticism to try to squeeze you into its mold, but don't be intimidated. When you stand for the truth, God stands with you. You need to have opinions based on a godly philosophy, and you can't be afraid to speak what you believe.

Also notice that the scripture goes a step beyond advising us to resist being conformed to this world; it tells us to be "transformed" by the renewing of our minds. The Greek word for transformed is *metamorphoō*, and it is the same root word for "metamorphosis" - the process by which a caterpillar morphs into a butterfly. In other words, you get total personal transformation by changing the way you think—which is why Christians need to have a godly philosophy that attempts to follow God's way of thinking. The apostle John said,

> *Love not the world, neither the things that are in the world. If any man love the world, the love of the Father is not in him. For all that is in the world, the lust of the flesh, and the lust of the eyes, and the pride of life, is not of the Father, but is of the world. And the world passeth away, and the lust thereof: but he that doeth the will of God abideth for ever.*

> *1 John 2:15-17*

When you are filled with love for this world and all that it offers, then there is no room left for loving God. "The lust of the flesh" is talking about all of the cravings people have for emotional and physical satisfaction: fame, adoration, sensual gratification, and the rest. God created us with a need to meet physical and emotional needs, but the world makes an idol of those drives—which forces out love of God.

Christian values are vastly different. The Apostle Paul said that he counted all of his worldly accomplishments as dung compared to knowing Christ—and Paul was one of the most accomplished Pharisees of his day. He didn't mean there is no value in natural achievements, just not in comparison with relationship to Christ.

A lot of Christians think it is over the top to say we are in a battle against the world system. They don't think the world is a bad place, and they don't think lost people are bad people. I agree that lost people aren't bad in the sense of being malicious, but many of them are promoting a moral system that is completely contrary to the Word of God—which is obviously detrimental to Christians.

I believe one of the worst mistakes being made by the body of Christ is trying to relate to the world too much. Christians are adopting the ways of the world in an attempt to relate to lost people. Now we have seeker-friendly churches that have reduced their sermons down to 10-minute pep talks and they have filled their services with entertainment. It's fine to try to relate to lost people, but not so much that the distinction between the world and Christianity is blurred. Unfortunately, I think the church has been negatively influenced by the world to a greater extent than we have been a positive influence on the world.

As Christians, we should be skeptical of the attitudes and opinions that prevail in the world. We should be different. Scripture refers to believers as "the church," which in the Greek literally means "called out ones." Being separate isn't about being physically isolated. It's about being detached in our philosophy and opinions, so just because people in the world have credentials, doesn't mean we should adopt their way of thinking. We shouldn't exalt the opinions of secular scientists, journalists, politicians, or other leaders above the Word of God—no matter what qualifications they have.

In 1999, many experts were predicting widespread computer problems when the date turned over to the year 2000. They were all claiming that the internal clocks in computers had not been programmed to count to 2000 after 1999, and that major computer malfunctions were going to result. The experts were predicting a major crisis that could lead to food, water, and power shortages, and they nicknamed the impending disaster Y2K.

Some Christians were saying that Y2K would be the beginning of the tribulation period. They thought the world was going to descend into total anarchy. People were stockpiling food and weapons—so they could kill their neighbors if they tried to steal their food. Preachers were actually teaching on self-defense and killing others "in the name of the Lord," in order to protect their families.

I didn't agree with what was being taught about Y2K for a number of reasons. First, the Lord had told me to go on television and my program wasn't scheduled to start until January 3, 2000. If everything that was predicted to happen actually occurred, then I wouldn't be on television, and so I just felt in my heart that Y2K wouldn't result in disaster. Second, I have a philosophy that God doesn't want me hoarding food while my neighbors starve, and He sure doesn't want me to kill them. Third, Christian philosophy says "give and it shall be given unto you"—it doesn't say withhold to save yourself.

I didn't have a word from God that Y2K was a hoax, but my Christian philosophy showed me that what was being said by the experts and taught in some churches was not consistent with Scripture. People were being motivated by fear, not faith. The Bible says,

Christian Philosophy

But the wisdom that is from above is first pure, then peaceable,
gentle, and easy to be intreated, full of mercy and good fruits,
without partiality, and without hypocrisy.

James 3:17

There was no joy in any of the so-called wisdom that people were sharing about Y2K. All of those teachings on hoarding food and weapons were extremism based on terror. It violated everything I knew from Scripture, so I rejected those teachings publicly way before Y2K was near.

Of course, the world didn't end, and nobody ran out of food or water. It was just like the craze in the late eighties when former NASA engineer Edgar Whisenant wrote the book *88 Reasons Why the Rapture Will Be in 1988.* The book sold 4.5 million copies, and generated a message that was preached throughout the world. When the Rapture didn't happen, Whisenant wrote three more books predicting why the Rapture would occur in 1989, 1993, and 1994.

It amazes me how gullible Christians can be, but they are that way because they don't have an established philosophy. They don't believe in the infallibility or inspiration of God's Word. They view the Bible as a book of wisdom containing vague suggestions that aren't necessarily relevant to their lives. But trusting in the accuracy and inspiration of Scripture will keep you from falling for all of the misinformation and fear that is being promoted by the world; having a Christian philosophy will protect you from all of that.

The world's wisdom is not working. People are taking pills to go to sleep, pills to wake up, and pills to get them through the day. Christians need something stronger to hold on to than "expert" opinions. God's Word has been proven true over thousands of years; it is reliable, and it needs to be the foundation of our lives.

We need to get to a place where we trust the Word of God more than the opinions of men. If an expert says something that contradicts God's Word, then we shouldn't exalt their opinion—no matter how many credentials they have. There's an old saying that if you don't stand for something, you'll fall for anything. Most people are living their lives in a state of flux; they bend with the wind and follow whatever opinions are dominating society. Trusting in the Word of God, on the other hand, will give you firmly established truths by which to anchor your life. You won't be tossed to and fro, carried about by every wind of doctrine, or by the cunning of men who lie in wait to deceive (Ephesians 4:14).

Everything in this world is going to pass away, but the Word of God will never fail. It is forever settled. Scripture says that God spoke the heavens and the earth into existence, and He holds all things together by His word. When you build your life on the Word of God, you are building on a foundation that will never fail.

I challenge you to begin reading the Bible with the openness to believe it is accurate and inspired. Read the New Testament and ask God, "Are these things true?" Ask God to reveal Himself to you. I believe that when you do, you will reach the same conclusions I have: The Word of God is true, it is accurate, and it is relevant to our lives. Once you start basing your philosophy on God's Word, it will completely change how you see and experience life.

Receive Jesus as Your Savior

Choosing to receive Jesus Christ as your Lord and Savior is the most important decision you'll ever make!

God's Word promises, "That if thou shalt confess with thy mouth the Lord Jesus, and shalt believe in thine heart that God hath raised him from the dead, thou shalt be saved. For with the heart man believeth unto righteousness; and with the mouth confession is made unto salvation" (Romans 10:9,10). "For whosoever shall call upon the name of the Lord shall be saved" (Romans 10:13).

By His grace, God has already done everything to provide salvation. Your part is simply to believe and receive.

Pray out loud: Jesus, I confess that You are my Lord and Savior. I believe in my heart that God raised You from the dead. By faith in Your Word, I receive salvation now. Thank You for saving me.

The very moment you commit your life to Jesus Christ, the truth of His Word instantly comes to pass in your spirit. Now that you're born again, there's a brand-new you.

Receive the Holy Spirit

As His child, your loving heavenly Father wants to give you the supernatural power you need to live a new life.

> For every one that asketh receiveth; and he that seeketh findeth; and to him that knocketh it shall be opened...how much more shall your heavenly Father give the Holy Spirit to them that ask him?
>
> Luke 11:10-13

All you have to do is ask, believe, and receive!

Pray: Father, I recognize my need for Your power to live a new life. Please fill me with Your Holy Spirit. By faith, I receive it right now. Thank You for baptizing me. Holy Spirit, You are welcome in my life.

Congratulations—now you're filled with God's supernatural power.

Some syllables from a language you don't recognize will rise up from your heart to your mouth. (1 Corinthians 14:14.) As you speak them out loud by faith, you're releasing God's power from within and building yourself up in the spirit. (1 Corinthians 14:4.) You can do this whenever and wherever you like.

It doesn't really matter whether you felt anything or not when you prayed to receive the Lord and His Spirit. If you believed in

your heart that you received, then God's Word promises you did. "Therefore I say unto you, What things soever ye desire, when ye pray, believe that ye receive them, and ye shall have them" (Mark 11:24). God always honors His Word—believe it!

Please contact me and let me know that you've prayed to receive Jesus as your Savior or be filled with the Holy Spirit. I would like to rejoice with you and help you understand more fully what has taken place in your life. I'll send you a free gift that will help you understand and grow in your new relationship with the Lord. Welcome to your new life!

About the Author

For over four decades, Andrew Wommack has traveled America and the world teaching the truth of the Gospel. His profound revelation of the Word of God is taught with clarity and simplicity, emphasizing God's unconditional love and the balance between grace and faith. He reaches millions of people through the daily *Gospel Truth* radio and television programs, broadcast both domestically and internationally. He founded Charis Bible College in 1994 and has since established CBC extension schools in other major cities of America and around the world. Andrew has produced a library of teaching materials, available in print, audio, and visual formats. And, as it has been from the beginning, his ministry continues to distribute free audio materials to those who cannot afford them.

To contact Andrew Wommack please write, e-mail, or call:

Andrew Wommack Ministries, Inc.
P.O. Box 3333
Colorado Springs, CO 80934-3333
E-mail: awommack@aol.com
Helpline Phone (orders and prayer):
719-635-1111
Hours: 4:00 AM to 9:30 PM MST

Andrew Wommack Ministries of Europe
P.O. Box 4392
WS1 9AR Walsall
England
E-mail: enquiries@awme.net
U.K. Helpline Phone (orders and prayer):
011-44-192-247-3300
Hours: 5:30 AM to 4:00 PM GMT

Or visit him on the Web at: www.awmi.net

The Believer's Authority

The controversial subject of the authority of the believer in Christ is widely discussed in the church today. Andrew Wommack brings a fresh perspective to this important spiritual truth that may challenge everything you've been taught including:

- If believers have been given authority, then when, how, and toward what should it be exercised? Don't assume the answer; discover the true battleground, and learn how to recognize the real enemy.
- Most people believe God created our enemy, Satan, but did He? Understanding the answer will set you free to exercise your authority as a believer.
- Is spiritual warfare, as taught in many churches today, valid? Can believers use their authority to fight the devil and his demons in the air, or is the real battle in the mind? The answer is an important prerequisite to winning spiritual battles.

Digging into the Scriptures, Andrew reveals the spiritual significance of your choices, words, and actions; and how they affect your ability to stand against the attacks of Satan and to receive God's best. Discover the powerful truths behind true spiritual authority and begin seeing real results.

Item Code: 1045-C, 6-CD album

Item Code: 1045-D, 5-DVD album (as recorded from television)

ISBN: 978-1-57794-936-7 Paperback

Available at bookstores everywhere or visit www.harrisonhouse.com

Other Teachings by Andrew Wommack

Spirit, Soul & Body

Understanding the relationship of your spirit, soul, and body is foundational to your Christian life. You will never truly know how much God loves you or believe what His Word says about you until you do. In this series, learn how they're related and how that knowledge will release the life of your spirit into your body and soul. It may even explain why many things are not working the way you had hoped.

Item Code: 318   Paperback
Item Code: 1027-C   4-CD album

The True Nature of God

Are you confused about the nature of God? Is He the God of judgment found in the Old Testament or the God of mercy and grace found in the New Testament? Andrew's revelation on this subject will set you free and give you a confidence in your relationship with God like never before. This is truly nearly-too-good-to-be-true news.

Item Code: 308   Paperback
Item Code: 1002-C   5-CD album

The Effects of Praise

Every Christian wants a stronger walk with the Lord. But how do you get there? Many don't know the true power of praise. It's essential. Listen as Andrew teaches biblical truths that will spark not only understanding but will help promote spiritual growth so you will experience victory.

Item Code: 309   Paperback
Item Code: 1004-C   3-CD album

God Wants You Well

Health is something everyone wants. Billions of dollars are spent each year trying to retain or restore health. So why does religion tell us that God uses sickness to teach us something? It even tries to make us believe that sickness is a blessing. That's just not true. God wants you well!

Item Code: 1036-C   4-CD album

Fast. Easy.
Convenient.

For the latest Harrison House product information and author news, look no further than your computer. All the details on our powerful, life-changing products are just a click away. New releases, e-mail subscriptions, testimonies, monthly specials—find it all in one place. Visit harrisonhouse.com today!

harrisonhouse